NEVER CRY HALIBUT

—— AND OTHER ——
ALASKA HUNTING & FISHING TALES

BJORN DIHLE

ALASKA
NORTHWEST
BOOKS®

Library of Congress Cataloging-in-Publication Data

Names: Dihle, Bjorn, author.
Title: Never cry halibut : and other Alaska hunting and fishing tales / Bjorn Dihle.
Description: Berkeley : Alaska Northwest Books, [2018]
Identifiers: LCCN 2017043435 (print) | LCCN 2018001441 (ebook) |
    ISBN 9781513260945 (ebook) | ISBN 9781513260921 (paperback) |
    ISBN 9781513260938 (hardcover)
Subjects: LCSH: Dihle, Bjorn. | Fishers--Alaska--Biography. |
    Hunters--Alaska--Biography.
Classification: LCC SH415.D54 (ebook) | LCC SH415.D54 A3 2018 (print) |
    DDC 639.2092 [B]--dc23
LC record available at https://lccn.loc.gov/2017043435

Edited by Kristen Hall-Geisler and Olivia Ngai

Cover art: Red monkey/Shutterstock.com; Meilun/Shutterstock.com;
Tribalium/Shutterstock.com; K N/Shutterstock.com
Interior graphics: ducu59us/Shutterstock.com; Red monkey/Shutterstock.com

Published by Alaska Northwest Books®
An imprint of

GRAPHIC ARTS
BOOKS®

GraphicArtsBooks.com

Graphic Arts Books
Publishing Director: Jennifer Newens
Marketing Manager: Angela Zbornik
Editor: Olivia Ngai
Design & Production: Rachel Lopez Metzger

CONTENTS

For my folks, Nils and Lynnette Dihle.

BLACKTAILS AND BROWN BEARS

MY DAD GREW UP in Sacramento reading stories about hunting and fishing in Alaska. In the early seventies, as strip malls and suburbia ate up the fields and woods surrounding his home, he persuaded my mom to move north. They were both kids, newly married and ripe for adventure. Alaska had untrammeled landscapes where people could wander, hunt, and fish where they pleased and not see another person for weeks. There were massive herds of caribou, and plenty of wolves hunting them. There were Dall sheep and thousands of miles of mountains. There were brown bears and blacktail deer, and to my dad it sounded like paradise.

Alaska didn't quite have the same ring for my mom.

"We'll try it for a year," my dad promised. "If we don't like it, we can always move back."

Reluctantly, and much to the disapproval of her family and friends, she agreed. Southeast Alaska seemed as far away as Russia, and between the bears, bugs, weather, and the price of a plane ticket, a trip north wasn't high on their circle's list of vacation destinations.

They loaded their tiny AMC Gremlin with a giant malamute and a high-strung Norwegian elkhound and drove out of the suburbs.

Following the Alaska Highway, they slowly motored through forests and mountains that seemed to stretch forever. In Fort John, British Columbia, the dogs rolled in something dead, making the final push to the Alaskan port of Haines a bit fragrant. Aboard the state ferry, they motored south down Lynn Canal, an expansive, storm-ridden fjord, with mountains towering up to seven thousand feet on both sides. Clouds clung to Admiralty Island's rainforest mountains as the ferry made a hard turn toward the small city of Juneau.

They settled there, cut off from the rest of the civilized world by a 1,500-square-mile icefield and a wilderness archipelago. It was late fall, the nastiest time of the year in Southeast. Having nowhere to live, they pitched a tent at a campground and slept with their dogs for nearly a month before they found a small rundown trailer. Their slate-gray rainy world was a hard adjustment for my mom, and a lifelong love-hate relationship with Southeast Alaska began as she watched snow creep down mountains and stared at a glacier in her backyard.

It was one thing to read about Alaskan hunting adventures and another thing to make your own. The forest and mountains, tangled and shrouded in constant storms, were nothing like the Sierras. My dad was armed with an ancient rifle with a bolt that was clunky and problematic. On one of his first ventures, he wandered through walls of alders, clawing brush, and gloomy old-growth forest to the top of a mountain to look for mountain goats. His excitement of finally going hunting in Alaska was not dampened by his inability to see more than a hundred feet in the foggy alpine. After spending the day sitting in the rain and snow, hoping a goat would appear out of the gray, and watching ravens glide in and out of view, he hurried down with an empty pack. After his being chilled and lightheaded from low blood sugar and wandering through a dark, dripping forest, a respect for how quickly even a day hunt could go awry was born.

A year later, having yet to harvest any Alaskan big game, my dad and his friend Joe skiffed across Stephens Passage to Admiralty Island for a fall deer hunt. Having heard stories of brown bears and frustrated with a gun that barely worked, he'd upgraded to a .338 Magnum. They anchored the boat offshore and carried a raft over popping seaweed and slick rocks. Ravens spoke their ancient language from spruce boughs, and eagles stared mutely out to sea. Higher on the beach in a sandy section, my dad knelt and studied large tracks unlike anything he'd seen. Brown bears. He knew this island, at a hundred miles long and twenty miles wide, was said to have the densest concentration of coastal grizzly bears in the world. Fresh deer tracks, tiny in comparison, wended along the high tide line. After agreeing on a return time, Dad pushed through the guard timber and stood on a well-worn bear trail paralleling the beach. Squinting into the sodden forest, he checked

A brown bear superimposed against the mountains of Admiralty Island.

his rifle, took a breath, and walked into the dark maze.

He traveled slowly over windfallen trees and through blueberry brush, alert and focused for any movement or sound. After hours of sneaking along without seeing a deer or meeting a bear, he came to the edge of a meadow and stopped to look and listen. The wind was still. A raven croaked, and an eagle cried its strange, haunted cry. Nothing unusual. He eased through shore pines and deciduous brush, and his rubber boot sunk into the muskeg. Slowly, he pulled his boot out, making a soft sucking sound. A flash of brown streaked across the meadow. Seeing it was a buck, he instinctively raised his rifle, and when the crosshairs rested on the blur of its vitals, he pulled the trigger. A moment later, the deer disappeared.

He hurried across the meadow, skirting sinkholes and small ponds, to where he'd last seen the deer. There was no snow for tracking, and after a long fruitless search for blood, he began to walk in circles, regretting taking such a rushed shot. More than an hour later, the light had faded, and the meeting time the friends had agreed on passed. Out of the corner of his eye, he noticed a raven and an eagle

Dad looking for deer in the mountains of northern Southeast Alaska. (Photo courtesy of Nils Dihle)

standing next to each other on a hummock. Investigating closer, he found a big buck, its antlers reddened from rubbing against alders, lying still atop wet moss and Labrador tea.

"It was weird," he told me years later, "seeing the eagle and the raven next to each other and that buck. The Tlingit have the two moieties, the eagle and the raven. Here I was a kid, green to their country, standing above the first deer I shot, in the company of an eagle and raven. I'm not sure what to make of it."

Not having time to haul the deer out, he gutted it and hung it from a tree, and raced back to Joe and the boat. They barely beat the darkness back to Juneau. Somehow Dad convinced my mom to accompany him to retrieve the deer the following morning.

Freedom is the word my mom still uses to describe the boat ride across Stephens Passage, but once on the shore of Admiralty Island, she realized the rules of civilization no longer meant anything. She peered at large bear tracks and piles of scat, and an unpleasant feeling came over her. Following Joe and my dad through the wet, claustrophobic woods, she stared up at the trees, wondering at the power of the rainforest and praying a bear didn't jump out of the brush.

Relieved to find the buck still hanging from a tree, the two friends packed the deer back to the beach. While paddling the raft out to the boat, they left my mom alone for a few minutes, and in those brief moments she vanished.

It's not rare for people to disappear in Southeast Alaska, so naturally, my dad's befuddlement slowly evolved into worry. Perhaps bears were as vicious as some claimed. Or maybe the local stories of shape-shifting fiends who lure people into the water or deep into the forest were true. Regardless, he'd lost his wife to the Alaskan wilds. Her family and friends would soon be sharpening their pitchforks and buying tickets north. The jungle of Admiralty Island might be a good place to hide out for a while.

The two friends began searching along the edge of the forest.

"Lynnette!" my dad yelled.

"I'm up here," she called from high in a tree, hidden in a maze of boughs.

"What are you doing up there? Is there a bear nearby?"

"Nope, just finding comfort in a tree," she said and began her way down.

Together the three skiffed toward Juneau, the jagged sentinel mountains guarding the icefield growing closer, the sharp wind on their faces.

Forty years later, my dad still brags about my mom's tree-climbing abilities. She still claims that she wasn't afraid of bears but was simply trying to get a better view.

Hunting stories are the oldest stories we have. My brothers and I listened to our dad's as we grew. We poked and examined the game he brought home to feed us. When we became old enough, he'd take us along, decreasing his odds of harvesting a deer but showing us the woods and how to hunt. When we were teenagers, we began to bring deer and our own stories home from the rainforest.

The first buck my dad shot was one of the biggest deer anyone in our family has harvested, not that it matters. What does matter is that more than forty years ago, amidst a rainforest of brown bears, my dad encountered something timeless and difficult to articulate in the presence of an eagle, a raven, and a deer. It is a gift he received and passed on to his sons.

SOOTY OBSESSION

I GREW UP IN JUNEAU, a city of thirty thousand surrounded by a wild expanse of temperate rainforest, mountains, and glaciers. Each summer, millions of salmon migrate up the rivers and streams of northern Southeast Alaska to spawn. Their flesh sustains some of the densest concentrations of bald eagles and brown bears in the world. Autumn brings more rain, blusters, and a loss of daylight that contribute to a widespread melancholy and even depression in locals. The darkness and storms of winter inspire many animals, people included, to migrate south or hibernate. Solace comes in the spring, when days grow longer and ridges and mountainsides come alive with the hooting of sooty grouse.

When I was a kid, I constantly dreamt of hooters. What did they look like? What did they taste like? Would I ever successfully hunt one? Each spring I listened to the sounds of their courtship booming off the steep, forested ridges and slopes and felt magnetically drawn. *Hooters*, the colloquial term for male sooty grouse, haunted much of my adolescence, so much so that I'd often wake at night in a cold sweat, my bedroom echoing with the sound of their mating calls.

When I was thirteen, my dad cut me loose with a bow, and I

set off to become a hunter. With my pal Thad, I thrashed through alders and devil's club—a very thorny and prolific member of the ginseng family—and hung off mountainsides trying to pinpoint the source of hooting. It seemed impossible to find a grouse high up in the thick tangle of branches, so we convinced ourselves it was just as likely they lived in dens on the ground. We investigated quite a few holes, one of which had been recently vacated by a bear. We never did spot a grouse; nonetheless, Thad tried to convince me we had accomplished something great.

"We're men now," he said toward the end of grouse season as we sat on the side of Eaglecrest Road waiting for my dad to pick us up.

"I wonder what a hooter looks like?" I said.

That summer, fall, and winter, I was haunted by hooters. I set about training one of our family's dogs, Buff, a young male Labrador retriever, to retrieve birds. Buff and I, armed with my bow, stalked several chickens I was raising—something my brothers still love to tease me about. While they frequently dispute who has shot bigger deer, they're always quick to give me credit for killing the biggest chicken.

Before long, Buff was retrieving chickens pretty well, and Dad helped me pick out a .22 rifle. While I was preparing for another season of thrashing through the woods and climbing into bear dens hoping to find a bird, I lucked out and befriended Tim, a seasoned grouse hunter old enough to have his driver's license. I told him about my inability to find any grouse the previous season despite investigating hundreds of likely looking holes in the earth, and he shook his head in disgust.

"They're up high in trees!" he said and, in a moment of compassion that would change my life forever, offered to take me along on a hunt. The following weekend, Tim, Buff, and I climbed a steep hill above a giant fjord. We plowed through brush and devil's club, clung to roots poking out from cliffs, and sunk into the decaying forest's floor. We clambered around a mossy cliff and came down on the sound of a booming grouse. For the next long while, I stared up at the dark canopy of branches while Tim scanned every nook and cranny in the maze of conifers.

"There he is!" he hollered. I rushed over but saw only branches and brush as Tim sighed impatiently. Finally, as the grouse boomed its mating call, I saw a dark chicken-sized bird bobbing its head in a web of branches. Tim offered me the shot, but I declined on the principle that I wouldn't pull the trigger until I spotted a bird myself. He shook his head and muttered something about the unlikeliness of that happening anytime soon. At the crack of the shot, the bird plummeted, and Buff plunged down the steep slope and disappeared into the brush. A short while later, he huffed his way back to us with the grouse held softly in his mouth. I examined its bluish-gray feathers and appreciated the patterns of its plumage as Buff rested a paw on me. Tim gave us a curious look, no doubt impressed with my dog even if he thought I was a fool. The three of us went hunting a lot that spring. I didn't spot a single hooter, but Buff retrieved every grouse we knocked out of a tree.

The woods became my refuge and Buff my constant companion and best friend. While other kids my age were dating, partying, and suffering from teen anxieties, I spent all my extra time hunting and exploring, mostly alone with my dog. We encountered wolves—one scrawny and hungry-looking loner tried its best to lure Buff away from my side. We surprised bears, some of whom huffed and clacked their teeth as we slowly backed away. On one occasion with Tim, we "accidentally" shot a big buck high on a mountain during a hike after school. We'd been walking along an alpine ridge late in the day when we unexpectedly encountered three deer in a ravine below. It just happened to be open season. Tim was one of those guys who believed in hiking with a rifle for fitness; he rarely entered the woods without packing. Together, we made a short stalk—not an easy task with a big Lab—and lined up on a big buck.

"This is a really bad idea," Tim said. We had no packs or knives, and getting down to the animal looked nothing short of heinous. I persuaded Tim it would be irrational not to shoot. We missed school the next day and showed up at home covered in deer blood, exhausted but happy.

Buff was a lovable fool and baby at home, but he became proud, focused, and riveted to my side whenever we went in the woods. We learned to hunt waterfowl together. When I'd make a lousy shot, Buff would dive underwater to catch wounded ducks or swim hundreds

Buff, my best pal growing up, on a lake in northern British Columbia.

of yards, despite my yelling, into choppy seas after a crippled bird. He'd return with a grouse even if it glided far down a mountain and work clumps of brush to jump birds in the early fall.

My obsession with sooty grouse hunting got so bad during my last two years of high school that I could think of little else once late winter came around. While my fellow students were at senior prom, Buff and I explored new territory loaded with hooters north of town. We bivouacked beneath a giant spruce, our shivering bodies pressed together, trying to fend off the cold, rain, and thoughts of brown bears during the long night.

After high school, I ventured beyond Juneau, and my shotgun and .22 collected dust in my parents' closet. While I tried to navigate college, work, and travel, I felt remorseful for leaving Buff behind. While I tried to figure out what to do with my life, I forgot how much our hunts and explorations meant to me. When I visited home, I could tell the strength of our bond had weakened. Buff became horribly arthritic, and I blamed myself for working him too hard. I cringed when he yelped while climbing the stairs.

For our last hunt, my little brother, Reid, and I took him grouse hunting. He gimped up the hill but happily retrieved the birds we shot. Afterward he could barely walk for days. Two autumns later, he could hardly walk at all. Reid would sometimes carry him to a duck blind. While he and Buff waited for a flock to fly overhead, he massaged Buff's atrophied, shivering hips. After a shot, when a duck plummeted from the slate-gray sky, for a moment Buff forgot how crippled he was, plunged into the water, and proudly retrieved the bird. That winter, while I was halfway around the world, I called my family from a dilapidated payphone. My dad told me he'd had to put Buff down.

Nearly a decade later, on the night before my thirtieth birthday, my older brother, Luke, called me on the phone.

"Come on, let's go hooter hunting tomorrow," he said. My .22 had disappeared, and it had been years since I thrashed through the woods after sooty grouse. There were errands and other things I needed to do, but I agreed to meet Luke at a trailhead at six in the morning. The hooting of the first grouse of the day brought back a flood of memories of Buff, Thad, and Tim, and sitting in class daydreaming about hooter hunting while popping out hundreds of devil's club thorns from my hands and forearms. Luke and I hiked through wet brush as the dark forest dripped and softly swooshed and creaked in the breeze.

"Got him," I said when I spotted a grouse high up, perched on a branch of a spruce tree. Luke, acting as a retriever, got under the tree the bird was in. I used his .22 and the grouse fell, its wings beating wildly, to the earth. We took turns shooting and retrieving until the early afternoon. Even though there were other grouse hooting nearby, we had four in the bag, more than enough for a birthday feast.

"Thank you, grouse; thank you, God," Luke said as he gutted the last bird of the day. Silently, I thanked Tim and Buff too.

THE FIRST DEER

WHEN WE WERE SIXTEEN YEARS OLD, my good pals Jesse
Walker and Ed Shanley and I skipped school to hunt Sitka blacktail
deer. We stumbled through drenched blueberry bushes, thorny
mazes of devil's club, and tangles of alders until we got to a mountainside covered in old-growth spruce and hemlock. Grabbing tree
roots, we clawed up a steep slope of moss, rocks, and loose soil. On
mountain benches, we crossed rain-swollen creeks running brown
and sank into skunk cabbage-covered muskegs.

"How am I supposed to keep up with an English mountaineer
and a savage?" Jesse muttered from the back as we emerged from
dark forest into a subalpine meadow. We rested atop a fallen tree to
feast on marble-sized blueberries. The rippling dark-blue swath of
Lynn Canal stretched to the north. The first of autumn's snow dusted
the Chilkat Range on the western horizon, and the gigantic white
summits of the Fairweather Range loomed beyond. To the east, 1,500
square miles of glaciers and mountains separated our community
from the expansive taiga of the Yukon. Admiralty Island, a wilderness of brown bears and rainforest, stretched a hundred miles to the
south. With purple-stained mouths, we spoke softly about the little

A big Sitka blacktail watches the author from high on a mountain on Admiralty Island.

we knew of hunting, mostly stories our dads had told us. I pointed Jesse in the direction of where we planned to camp.

"This is the last time I'm climbing a mountain with you guys," he growled as Ed and I hurried ahead to get in an evening hunt. Ed and I crested the top of the mountain and glassed a valley. To our surprise, a deer placidly grazed on deer lettuce and blueberry leaves below. With pounding hearts, we stalked as close as cover allowed.

"Too far!" I whispered as Ed and I looked at an unsuspecting buck less than a hundred yards away. "Do you think you could hit it?"

"No, too far!" Ed agreed. The buck's antlers splayed out beyond his ears. We cursed under our breath and tried to figure out how to sneak closer. We belly crawled a few yards more before the deer snorted and disappeared into the brush.

The sun was sinking toward the summit of Nun Mountain when we stumbled upon a large, blond, hairy beast snoring beneath a jack pine. The creature groaned, roared, and shook itself. For a second, I nearly readied my rifle before Jesse rose to his full height, eyeing us malevolently. After a brief conference, Ed grabbed the other rifle and strolled off toward where we had last seen the buck. Jesse and I snuck over to the edge of a bowl and glassed the grassy stretches.

The Chilkat Range glistened red above the murky-blue Pacific. In the last moments of shooting light, I noticed Jesse flapping his arms like he was trying to fly. Upon closer examination, I understood him to be gesturing at the valley below. Two hundred yards away, a deer cautiously emerged from the dark forest. There was something phantasmal in its form as it tentatively moved through the failing light. I had my grandfather's ancient .308. Its bolt didn't work well, and in all its years of existence, it had only killed one or two animals. I belly crawled a few yards closer and awkwardly clanked a round into the chamber. Through the old four-power scope, I rested the crosshairs on the tiny image of the deer's chest. It seemed impossibly far away. I hardly noticed the report of the shot.

"I missed!" I told my wild-eyed friend after he charged over. Staring down into the gloom, we saw no evidence of a deer or movement. The last of the alpenglow faded from the glacier-covered mountains. "I wish I hadn't shot. I missed, but we should go take a look to make sure."

We felt our way down a steep, slippery slope of deer lettuce, occasionally sliding. Jesse stopped and squinted into the darkness.

"I think the deer's lying there," he said.

The deer, a fork-horn buck, lay staring at the forest twenty yards away. I sat, clunked a bullet into the chamber, put the crosshairs on the base of his skull, and pulled the trigger.

Overwhelmed, Jesse ran to the deer, dodging kicking hooves and shaking antlers, and lay atop the animal as its life left it. Ed, hearing the shots, made his way down to us. Together, the three of us gutted and hung the deer in a small spruce. Covered in deer blood, we slept on heather and deer lettuce next to a fire that night.

The smell of sweat, deer, blueberry leaves, decay, spruce, and hemlock accompanied us down the mountain the following day. Our packs sagged with the weight of the meat. The wind rustled trees, and condensation dripped from branches. That night we fried heart and barbecued ribs. None of us had ever eaten a meal so fine.

MY BEST TROPHY

I CAN IMAGINE FEW THINGS more terrible or wonderful than being a parent, particularly a mom. My own mother was abducted from California to Alaska and then forced to live with a wild husband and three savage sons. Imagine coming home from work to see a bloody pelt on the kitchen counter and your six-year-old son gnawing a boiled squirrel. Maybe it's not that weird for Alaskan mothers, but for a young woman who grew up in Sacramento, it must have been disorienting at best. Ermine, marten, and a variety of rodent soups—my mom was always in for a surprise when we cooked dinner. The house, with piles of bones and antlers strewn about, seemed like a Neanderthal clan's cave crossed with a hunting lodge. For the most part, she bore the horror quietly and late at night, as she stared up at the aurora dancing or through sheets of rain in the inky blackness, dreamed of ridding her house of dead animals. This seemingly simple task—a basic human right in other parts of the country—became as epic a quest as Frodo's journey to Mordor in *The Lord of the Rings*.

Growing up, I didn't sympathize much with her. I couldn't fathom why anyone wouldn't want their house to smell like a rutting buck or a salmon spawning ground. Why change your clothes or take a bath when you'd be dirty again a few hours later? Up until the point Nintendo was created, there was nothing cooler than pelts, bones, and stuffed game animals. Forget Disneyland. A trip to visit a taxidermist—even an amateur whose road-killed critter mounts looked like they'd suffered horribly botched plastic surgery from the shaky hands of an Amazonian witch doctor—was once my happiest place on earth. Each antler, hide, and bone was fought over. My mother's greatest victory was excommunicating our dad's sheep and goat mounts from the living room. Over the years, after my brothers and I left home, she reclaimed her house. Only one dead animal memento remains—a stuffed ten-inch golden trout I caught with a worm when I was a small kid.

Back then, my friends all seemed to have Nintendos, and when I visited them and played *Super Mario, The Legend of Zelda*, and *Street Fighter*, it felt like heaven. It was even more fun than looking through the stack of *Playboys* one of my friends' dads left out. Who cares about girls or being in the outdoors when you can make an Italian dwarf do flips onto a psychedelic mushroom? When I tried to convey my passion for video games and begged for a Nintendo of my own, my folks were oddly quiet. Screaming, throwing fits, and running away for a few hours didn't do much good either. Finally they had enough.

"Save up your money, and you can buy your own," my dad said. So began an era of economic fortitude. No more Bazooka gum. No more packs of Upper Deck sports cards. No more fantasy lead figurines. My will was unbreakable. The Nintendo would be mine.

More than a year after I began saving, my family was spending the summer in Bozeman, Montana. I counted out my money and did the math. It was time! Before taking me to the store, my dad suggested we go fishing and camping for the weekend.

"Did I ever tell you about golden trout? There's hardly any, and they only live high in mountain lakes," he said reverently as he drove his three sons up a winding dirt road. Soon, he had me believing that catching a golden trout would be as unique and spectacular as seeing Sasquatch. My fascination with dead animal mementos and trophies came back with a vengeance. What if an asthmatic porker like me somehow managed to climb through the mountains and, by the wildest twist of fate, was able to hook the El Dorado of the trout world? Would it be possible to manifest that great moment forever and get it mounted by a taxidermist? The very thought of torturing my mom and solidifying my greatness as an outdoorsman sent shivers down my spine.

The two-mile hike was akin to Amundsen's trek to the South Pole, but the thought of golden trout spurred me on. Finally, when we stood at the edge of a blue-water alpine lake, I put a worm on a hook and cast out near a partly submerged log. When my red-and-white bobber went under, I thought I'd won the lottery. The trout, golden colored with dark bars and spots, was a beauty. On the hike out, I wrestled with the most difficult existential question I'd yet to face: Nintendo or stuffed trout. By the time we made it home, I asked Dad if we could get the fish stuffed. He'd already carefully placed the tiny trout in wet leaves, and we beelined to a friendly taxidermy shop. I immediately regretted handing over the money. It would be years, perhaps forever, before I'd have enough money to buy a Nintendo.

My parents love that golden trout. It's the only trophy I've kept from the woods, other than the Dall sheep horns on my bookshelf. My three young nieces sometimes suggest I upgrade and get a herring mounted for my next trophy. This offers me an excuse to ramble off a "when I was your age" story with a moral that neither they nor I can make sense of. Often these backwoods parables end with some wisdom like "...and that's why you should never pet a humpy salmon when it's spawning," or "...and that's why you should not dress up in a deer costume while hunting on Admiralty Island."

The three sisters are lucky to have parents who make sure they get plenty of time out in nature. One of my favorite things to do is walk in the woods or go fishing with them and see how excited they get. When their dad, Luke, decided to take Kiah, his eldest, sooty grouse hunting for the first time, I was lucky enough to be invited along. Most folks call these grouse "hooters," after the males who perch high in conifer trees and hoot to establish territory and attract mates. Luke and Kiah, with me and Dad tagging along, made an early season foray into the snowy mountains. Just the day before, there were a couple lovelorn fellows reciting their monosyllabic poetry in a winter storm, but on this day, the forest was quiet other than the

Luke and Kiah with a sooty grouse.

wind, ravens, and a hairy woodpecker. On the last day of the season, Luke, Kiah, and I waded through brush toward a mountainside we hoped had a few birds. I'm pretty sure Luke and I were more excited than Kiah. Deer poop and tracks crisscrossed a muskeg. A network of game trails spread through a forest of towering Sitka spruce and western hemlock. Snowy mountain summits appeared through breaks in green foliage. Clumps of wolf hair hung in brush, and piles of bear scat lay at the edge of verdant avalanche paths. Soon the deep booming of grouse brought the forest even more to life. Luke began to get farther and farther ahead. Kiah didn't stop or complain; she simply hiked faster. As she tunneled through a maze of devil's club, she stared back with a confused look.

"This is what you guys do for fun?" she asked. I shrugged and said yeah, suddenly self-conscious.

Luke made a great spot on the first bird, but with just a tiny bit of it visible, it was the sort of shot only an expert marksman could make. The next bird offered a similar perspective, so I suggested Luke shoot it. As we were lacking a dog, I did the fetching. Kiah held the bird and studied it with mixed emotions, saying how beautiful it was over and over again. We moved on to the next hooter, which was silhouetted and quite a bit closer. Luke helped Kiah find a rest. At the sound of the shot, the bird plummeted. We found it beneath a giant root wad. Kiah stroked its feathers and held it tenderly before gutting and skinning it. At Luke's encouragement—and the thought of how I might have to wait almost a year before having another delicious grouse dinner—I added another hooter to the bag on the hike down.

I followed my brother and his daughter, listening to other grouse hoot and thinking about how lucky I was to share the day with them. Kiah held her dad's hand as we hiked along the edge of the ocean. She'd gotten dozens of devil's club thorns, a few good scratches, and her feet were a bit sore, but she'd never admit it. Watching her with my brother brought back memories of the golden trout. That tiny fish may not be a four-by-four Sitka blacktail, or forty-inch sheep, or fifty-pound king salmon, but to this day, it's the greatest trophy I have.

FISH TERRORS

"BITE MY FLY!" I woke up screaming. My girlfriend, MC, tried to calm me as I hyperventilated and shook an imaginary rod. Perhaps I inherited fish terrors from my good friend and commercial fishing captain, Joe Craig—while we were at anchor, he'd often wake me screaming about fishing in his sleep—or maybe my subconscious was trying to work through the emotional aftermath of all the fish that had ignored my lures or gotten away.

"Stop!" MC yelled as I nearly hit her. I was mimicking throwing my rod down in disgust. "Calm down. You had a bad dream. Was it the Arctic grayling this time?"

"No, it was that pike again. He just swam there, smiling with his big eyes and teeth, laughing at me as I tried everything I could to catch him."

"You need to get help. You have a problem."

"What's my problem?"

"Something bad. It's more than just being a lousy fisherman," she said. She was still proud of the seventy-pound halibut she'd caught with my dad a few weeks prior. Though she'd once been a vegetarian, her Facebook profile picture for the next seven months would be of her and a dead halibut. She even started giving experienced longliners advice on how to catch the big ones. She got even cockier when Troy Leatherman, the editor of *Fish Alaska Magazine*, asked to use the picture for a cover shot.

That morning, while drinking coffee, I read an article in the most recent issue of *Today's Angler Psychology Magazine* that offered a pretty good explanation on why I had fish terrors. It described a recent study that showed 81 percent of fishermen exhibit symptoms of The Fish Or Me (TFOM) syndrome. Doctors say the neurosis results from the feeling that one's father or boat captain has at one time or another considered murdering them for not setting the hook properly or losing a fish. Those suffering from TFOM often have fishing performance anxiety issues and catch less fish than the 19 percent of the individuals who are deemed healthy. Finally my inability to catch fish made sense. It wasn't that I lacked skills or commitment, or hadn't listened to my dad as he painstakingly tried to teach me. It was because of TFOM. Now that I had identified the root of my problem, I felt confident I could be cured.

I traced my fish terrors back to a particular fly-fishing incident with my dad in the mountains above Bozeman. Trembling, I realized I would have likely become a lawyer, doctor, or politician if my life hadn't been hijacked that day. Instead, I became a degenerate woods-man and a lousy fisherman. The history leading up to the incident is a bit foggy but begins in the summer of 1989 or 1990. My family had driven from our home in Alaska to Montana so my folks could go back to college. We arrived at Bozeman when Robert Redford was filming *A River Runs Through It*. At a summer camp, I met a boy who claimed his dad was a stunt man in the film.

"What sort of stunts?" I asked. I'd never fly-fished, but it didn't seem like an activity involving too much danger.

"Fly-fishing stunts," he said. As soon as Dad put a rod in my hands, I realized the kid was telling the truth. Fly-fishing was dangerous. There were beavers to contend with, crashing brush when I tried to free a fly from a tree, lightning storms, and tangles that couldn't be untangled. Most of all, there were the consequences of losing a fish in front of my dad.

It was at Hyalite Creek in the mountains above town, while

A spring king salmon. (Photo courtesy of MC Martin)

hunting for brook trout, where I credit the birth of my neurosis. After hours of following Dad through thick brush with an impossibly long fly rod snagging on everything possible and tangling my reel as I cried, Dad shoved me into a creek.

"That looks like a good spot for a fish," he whispered, gesturing at a slow-moving section of the creek. "Cast over there."

After hooking a tree once and splashing the water twice, I managed to get the fly near where Dad pointed. A few moments later, a fish sucked it down. I was so flattered, I didn't think to set the hook. The fly floated free, and what sounded like a wounded grizzly bear made me realize that if I didn't catch this fish, I'd likely be mauled. Awkwardly, I cast again.

"Now!" Dad roared. I pulled the fly out of the fish's mouth with a violence more fitting for a mixed martial arts match. I was sure now: it was the fish or me. Sobbing and trying to make peace with death, I whipped my fly back into the creek and offered a pathetic prayer to the fish gods. The next moment, the fly was sucked down, my reel zinged out line, and my dad's inner berserker came out as he yelled, thrashed the water, and howled. A minute or so later, I pulled in a fifteen-inch grayling, a fish I had never seen and had no idea existed in Montana. Its iridescent scales and giant, sail-shaped dorsal fin made me forget how close I came to dying. Dad, knowing how rare Arctic grayling were in Montana, helped me gently release the fish. Watching it swim away, I wasn't sure if it was the fish or me that was more traumatized from the experience.

I admitted I had a problem and discovered where my neurosis originated. Now I needed to do something to end my fish terrors and become a better fisherman. But what? Should I fly to India, find an ashram, and meditate until fish no longer haunted my dreams? Perhaps there are doctors out there willing to medicate me antifi-shotics? Or a twelve-step program for fisherman suffering from TFOM?

"Hello, my name is Bjorn Dihle. I've not had fish terrors for a week now."

But what would haunt my dreams in the place of fish? I doubted there was anything out there as satisfying to be haunted by. Nothing as simple and magical as their lives and stories shrouded beneath the water. The dirty truth of the matter was that I cherished my fish demons. I miss fishing in Hyalite Creek, and I think about that first grayling more than is healthy. Waking up screaming is a small price to pay for having been lucky enough to go fishing.

MOUNTAIN OF MEMORIES

THERE ARE MANY GREAT THINGS about civilization—reality television, french fries, and a seemingly infinite number of back-hair waxing products, for example. I try to appreciate the advantages of living in the twenty-first century, but sometimes it gets a little much. On a recent August day, while in a giant shopping mall, I was suddenly overcome with an intense feeling of hopelessness. Near the toddler's clothing fashions, I fought the urge to crash a shopping cart into a pretentiously dressed mannequin. When did little kids begin caring about fashion? Whatever happened to the days when they were content wearing burlap sacks and chasing animals, rolling in mud and eating worms? And what was with all these skinny, anatomically correct mannequins with their chiseled abs and smug smiles? Give me realism; give me mannequins with beer guts, fat butts, crooked noses, lopsided skulls, varicose veins, crooked spines, and blemished skin. I had the feeling something other than me was trying to manufacture my reality. I was nearing the aisle dedicated solely to no-tears pet shampoo and conditioner when I had the sudden desire to flee into the wild.

"I have to go hunting," I told my girlfriend, MC, as we put away groceries when I got home.

"You just got back yesterday. There's still deer blood rotting in your hair!" she said. "And you're leaving in a few days with your brothers to go sheep and caribou hunting."

Everyone knows it's bad luck to shower during hunting season, but MC is always busting my chops about it. It might be our biggest point of contention; well, that and she gets all weird and irrational at the beginning of each hunting season when I stage a few harmless pagan rituals and become the Wildermann—a furry man-beast with an insatiable appetite for blood—for a night. I don't see what the big deal is. It's just a chance to blow off a little steam, get dressed up in furs, and run around the neighborhood howling and chasing dogs, cats, and children with a torch and stone ax.

"You can take the jungle out of the tiger, but you can't take the tiger out of the jungle," I whispered, staring off into the distance.

"I think you mean you can take the tiger out of the jungle, but you can't take the jungle out of the tiger," MC said.

"I'm a writer! I know what I'm saying!"

Whenever I get to feeling too domestic, I crack a beer, pick up a hammer, and start hitting two-by-fours. My pounding succeeded in annoying MC so much she kicked me out of the house. Soon, I was happily climbing through the rainforest, wading through devil's club, and stuffing my face with marble-sized blueberries and huckleberries. A black merlin winged along the edge of a meadow, hunting songbirds. A sooty grouse flew up into a small hemlock tree then looked down just feet away. I followed a well-used deer trail into the subalpine of a mountain I've hunted for two decades.

Fifteen Augusts ago, when I was seventeen and my little brother, Reid, was thirteen, we followed the same deer trail along the edge of an alpine slope. I spied a deer through the maze of underbrush. Hearts hammering and skin tingling, we belly crawled to the edge of the bushes and peered up. A beautiful fork-horn grazed above three does. I passed Reid my rifle. He crawled a few feet forward. As if he'd done it a thousand times before, he chambered a round, took a rest, and shot his first buck.

The clouds dissipated, revealing ocean and the mountains of Admiralty Island and the Chilkoot Range stretching into the blue

Reid in the alpine of Admiralty Island. (Photo courtesy Luke Dihle)

horizon. The vision never failed to remind me how lucky I was to live in Southeast Alaska. When I was thirteen, I first climbed the mountain with my dad and took in this haunting view. My dad patiently waited as I struggled up the slippery slopes with all the stealth and grace of an exhausted freight train. The following morning, after he tried to rouse me from my sleeping bag to brave the rain and fog, I heard a shot. I still remember the smell and touch of that young buck, the first deer I ever "helped" butcher and carry off a hill.

Climbing a steep, slippery slope, I spotted a deer in a stand of stunted trees. I froze, then slowly raised my rifle and looked through the scope. No antlers. I waited until it walked off, and I hiked to a bench my family had used as a camp spot. I dropped a small tent and sleeping bag before heading off to glass a couple different bowls. A red-tailed hawk shrieked and harassed an immature bald eagle lazily circling in the blue sky. I crept up to the edge of a draw, lay on my belly, and waited for dusk to come. Like magic, two does appeared on the opposite side.

I remembered when I was fifteen, my older brother, Luke, and I saw a nice fork-horn in this same draw. We were green—Luke missed twice, and I proceeded to shoot the ground in front of me. On Luke's third shot, the fleeing deer stumbled then disappeared. With ringing ears, we looked at each other in shock. In our rush to find the deer, I fell down a steep slope toward a cliff but miraculously slammed into the one stunted tree growing from the edge. Luke chose a better route down, and together we stood in awe over his first deer.

Dusk was nearing as I crawled away from the two does and crept back to camp. A small deer flickered inside a maze of jack pines. A moment later, it was gone. I passed the rock where, when I was seventeen, my friend Orion had lined up on his first buck at just twenty yards. After panting for five minutes—the deer oddly unaware—he whispered, "Should I?" There was the bowl where I've spent hours with my dad and brothers glassing. There was the spot where I accidentally shot two bucks one foggy, rainy morning. There was the ridge where that spike had been bedded down two Septembers ago. There was the ravine where that little fork-horn had been at the edge of in late September. There was the bowl where, with my friends Jesse and Ed, I took my first buck when we were sixteen. Reid and I had taken many more out of the same spot since.

It was near dark by the time I made it to camp. I was considering crawling into my sleeping bag when a deer emerged from the forest four hundred yards away. In the low light, I couldn't tell whether it was a buck or doe. I grabbed my pack and crept along the forest's edge, careful to make sure I didn't silhouette myself. Through a break in the trees, thirty yards away, two deer stood. One had antlers. I quietly worked my bolt, brought the rifle to my shoulder, and fired. In the darkness, I found the buck lying nearby in deer lettuce, heather, and false hellebore. I lay my gun down and rested a hand on his warm body as the last of the crimson sunset disappeared behind the Chilkat Mountains. After gutting and splitting his brisket, I partly skinned his hindquarters and broke his pelvis so the meat would better cool. By Southeast standards, it was a hot night. I wedged a few sticks in his rib cage to air him out and then hoisted him the best I could in a stunted tree. I tied my sweat-drenched shirt on a foreleg in the hopes of scaring off bears.

The black merlin was hunting the meadow as I packed the buck out the following morning. Nearby, a fawn leapt out of the brush then looked me over for a minute before disappearing into the old-growth forest. A goshawk hurled itself between trunks and branches of giant hemlock and spruce trees. It paused midflight and gripped the vertical trunk of a large hemlock with its talons when it saw me. It spread its wings apart and stared, its red eyes burning, then leapt back into flight. The pack, filled with fifty pounds of premium venison, bit into my shoulders, but it was a weight I was happy to carry.

At home, MC had filled the bathtub with warm bleach water and left out a wire brush, paint thinner, and waterproof sandpaper. On the sink was a bottle of the latest and greatest hair removal product she'd bought for me. It wouldn't work anyway—the hair on my back only comes out thicker and coarser. You can take the jungle out of the tiger, but you can't take the tiger out of the jungle.

RETURN OF THE PRODIGAL FISHERMAN

MY DAD DID EVERYTHING RIGHT to raise his three sons to be fishermen. He taught us to spin cast, troll, fly-fish, and halibut fish during outings that generally involved hours of untangling lines and existential crises. Quite frequently on these fishing expeditions, I was convinced I was tottering on the edge of hypothermia and perhaps even death. When I whimpered, my dad would try to set me straight.

"You don't know how lucky you are," he'd say over the pouring rain and howling wind, a string of cohos over his shoulder, me sniveling and shivering in tow. "When I was your age, I walked miles to the dam on the Sacramento River to catch twelve-inch hatchery trout."

Dad's diligent, often frustrating labor paid off for the most part. His love for fishing passed on to my two brothers, who put in their hours each year. My older brother, Luke, enjoys fishing so much, he'll even cast for humpies and chums—he eats them too. My little brother, Reid, told me the other day he might enjoy fishing more than hunting, which is the most controversial statement I've ever heard him make. Every family has its black sheep, and in regards to fishing, I guess it was me.

My career as a fisherman began as bright and hopeful as my

brothers'. I tangled just as many lines—and perhaps even more. I got pretty good at being hypothermic, something to this day I'm proud of. I got in the way when my dad was trying to net, contributing to the loss of several king and coho salmon. I massacred fillet jobs, cut myself, and broke knives. I dropped valuables over the edge of the skiff and lost hundreds of dollars' worth of lures and gear. I'm not sure if my dad was relieved or disappointed when I declined his offers to go fishing during my teenage years. Soon my mom put my poles in the mysterious, carnivorous underbelly of the house. They vanished, along with all other outdoor gear that had ever been stored there.

Somehow, perhaps out of pity or desperation on the part of the captains who hired me, I started crewing on a number of commercial fishing boats. Now I was getting paid to be soaking wet and hypothermic, plus tangle lines, lose gear, and get in the way. Some of my favorite times were based out of Elfin Cove, longlining on the *Njord* for halibut in Cross Sound with Joe and Sandy Craig. The first May I worked for them was rife with gale warnings and stormy seas.

"I hired a Jonah!" I heard Joe muttering as we tossed about, trying to snag the buoys attached to one side of our set. The fishing was slow, so the three of us got to spend a lot of time yelling, swearing, and bonding. One of my duties was to relay directions and curses between Joe, who was situated in the stern, and Sandy, who was driving in the wheelhouse. It was like the commercial fishing version of the game Telephone.

"Look," Sandy had warned me on the first day we met, "when we're out fishing, you're going to hear Joe and me yell a lot of horrible things at each other. We still love each other; it just gets a little stressful at times. I'm sorry that you'll often be the go-between for the two of us."

I didn't mind though. Whenever we snagged a set on the rocky sea floor, I got a chance to blow off some steam and work on my improv, adding a little extra drama and profanity to their warnings at each other.

One afternoon, after we'd finished up with their halibut quota, we decided to take the skiff out to Port Althorp and troll for a king. The sudden transition from working with hundreds of hooks to just one left me with that same drowsiness I got toward the end of my days of going fishing with my dad. I was half-asleep when Joe and Sandy started yelling, the line on the reel began zinging, and the spasmodic pole was shoved into my hands. They'd trolled these waters for nearly forty years and caught thousands of kings, but for the next five minutes, with all their whooping and hollering, I could have believed this was their first.

"There's nothing better in life than catching king salmon," Joe said as we admired the rainbow-scaled salmon. We barbecued a chunk on a cedar plank, and I embarked on a path of seafood snobbery.

Besides getting wet and hypothermic, tangling lines, and getting in the way of angry captains, there were other benefits to commercial fishing. A lot of folks who normally wouldn't have thought much of me but suffered some romantic notions about commercial fishermen gave me much more respect than I deserved. I used my "Don't worry, I'm a commercial fisherman" trick to fool MC, who'd recently moved to Alaska, into hanging out with me. She denies it, but I think dating a commercial fisherman was on her bucket list. I got her hooked on seafood, and she hasn't been able to shake me since. Things got a bit rough when she discovered the true extent of my fishing skills.

"I can't wait to catch my first salmon!" she exclaimed when she visited in Elfin Cove. On a day off, I borrowed Joe and Sandy's skiff and took her to the head end of Port Althorp. Thousands of humpies were milling and splashing in the shallows, waiting for the tide to rise so they could swim upriver and spawn. Armed with a quarter-ounce pixie, I was sure she'd have a fish the first cast. Two hours later, we were still fishless. She looked at me, quietly judging, as humpies leaped out of the water in every direction. On the way back to Elfin Cove, I pointed out whales, sea otters, a derelict cannery, glaciers, and mountains, but she seemed uninterested. Bob-o, one of the most hardcore fisherman in the Cross Sound fleet, tried to make me feel better.

"Ah, I can't catch anything with a fishing pole either," he said, which I appreciated even though I highly doubted it.

"Look, MC, commercial fishing and sport fishing are two different arts," I tried to explain.

"Maybe someone else could help me catch my first salmon?" she teased.

A wild Southeast Alaskan king salmon.

The next year for her birthday, she wanted a salmon pole and to go fishing and kayaking. I paddled a double kayak out to an island as she trolled a Flying-C with a focus so intense I was at first amused and then frightened. After three hours of paddling and no fish, she continued casting while I set up the tent and gathered beach wood for a fire. Finally she caught a small Dolly Varden, and was satiated enough to enjoy some birthday cake. We went fishing a few more times, catching sea slugs, sculpins, and small Dolly Varden before I knew had to go to my dad and ask a favor.

"I think MC might leave me if she doesn't catch a salmon soon. Do you think you could take her the next time you go out?" I asked. He happily agreed, and of course they went out and caught a pile. When she came home that night, we cooked a salmon dinner and put the rest of her catch in a brine.

"I caught a smoker load!" She beamed. "I can take you fishing your next day off, if you want."

I began to steal out in the predawn hours, borrowing her rod and then sneaking it back before she woke. These forays were partially inspired by wounded pride, but I soon found myself enjoying standing on the ocean's edge, casting in the morning solitude, and quietly chanting, "I am not a Jonah. I am not a Jonah."

I rarely caught much, but folks seemed more at ease around me now that I'd picked the rod back up. My dad and brothers started inviting me out on their skiff to go to their secret halibut holes; old friends called wanting to know if I wanted to go try for some cohos.

In late July of 2012, with my brothers and MC, we tried for halibut in Lynn Canal. The ocean stretched blue and undulated gently, mountains rose to nearly seven thousand feet in a couple miles, and glaciers cut through rainforest like giant frozen rivers. A pod of Dall's porpoises played with our skiff, bumping lines as we jigged. Humpback whales plied the waters with gargantuan baleen-plaited mouths spread wide. Bald eagles, gulls, sea ducks, and a host of other birds revolved in and out of vision.

"We don't know how lucky we are." My dad's words escaped me as I quelled the sudden urge to tangle my line and throw my pole overboard. MC and my brothers didn't reply. They were too busy waiting for a fish to strike.

MEAT HUNTER'S CREED

I'M LARGELY GOVERNED BY my nobility paunch—the new and politically correct term for a belly—so naturally I'm a meat hunter. Given the opportunity, I shoot the tastiest-looking animal available, often the smaller buck or bull in the mix. My brothers like to say my lack of trophies has something to do with my skills as a hunter, which is 100 percent bullarky. The skill and wit of a man with as much nobility as I have should never be questioned. If Boone and Crockett had a record for the most passed-up trophies, I'm sure I'd be a contender. Take the 2014 opener for Sitka blacktails. I passed on a massive four-by-three buck to take a chunky fork-horn instead. A few moments later, my older brother, Luke, shot the mammoth.

"I could have shot the big deer, but he didn't look as tasty," I said after we gutted and propped the deer to cool.

"You didn't even see him! He was off to your side," Luke said, still ecstatic for some reason.

Contrary to many folks' beliefs, meat hunters are neither dim-witted nor lazy, nor do we shoot anything that moves. In fact, meat hunting is one of the most ancient forms of art. Someday soon, high-brow museums will devote large exhibits to the subject. Ironically dressed intellectuals smoking cigarettes and drinking kombucha will browse the displays.

"Hmm, yes, the caribou hunting painting is so post-archaic garde."

"Hmm, yes, primitive but bold."

"I only see a bunch of colors and squiggly lines."

"You're not looking deep enough."

As a meat hunter concerned with my nobility paunch and the paunches of those I care for, I have great respect for the animals I harvest. My dad, in raising three half-feral sons, reiterated certain lessons over and over.

"Know where your gun is shooting before you go into the woods. When you see the right animal, take a good rest. Don't rush. Make a clean shot. It's better to watch an animal run off healthy than to miss and wound it," he told us as we learned to handle the responsibility of being hunters. I soon found that killing as swiftly and humanely as possible was only part of becoming a good hunter.

The next step, one my family claims took me a while to master, was proper care of meat. "Beasting" is a form of intelligence yet to be recognized by modern-day psychology that I possess a great deal of. Its application is best suited for making messes, lifting heavy objects, and involuntarily emitting animal sounds during social engagements. While beasting can help you in many situations, it works in your disfavor if applied to gutting and butchering an animal.

"You've got to keep the salad and the meat separate," Luke said when I kept bringing home meat seasoned with vegetation, hair, and dirt. Not being much of a salad guy anyway, I quickly learned what a big difference correctly field dressing meant for the quality of the meat. I began treating game like red gold, taking great care to quickly and neatly gut, butcher, and cool an animal. I learned tricks from my dad, brothers, and friends to make it easier, such as sawing open the brisket to easily remove the guts, which minimizes the chance of spilling the acidic contents of the stomach into the viscera and spoiling meat. Meticulously cutting away any blood-shot meat and avoiding scent glands. Keeping the heart—and the quarter with evidence of sex attached if the law requires it—in separate game bags. Always setting a quarter down on a garbage or game bag rather than the ground. Using pillowcases or some sort of game bags with

A late-season Sitka blacktail.

fabric impenetrable to fly eggs during warmer months. Keeping meat dry, aerated, and cool. I learned that every ounce of flesh on an animal, if cared for properly, has a use and can be delicious; even sinewy scraps are great for canning, burger, or sausage.

For many folks, me included, hunting is easier and more enjoyable than cooking. During a lot of my teens and early twenties, I'd kill an animal, bring it home, and go to town on chunks of meat much like a bear or wolf. Thinking about those times makes me nostalgic and brings back the memory of one November when I subsisted almost entirely on caribou and coffee (it seemed to make sense at the time, but in retrospect, I do not recommend this diet). A girl, perhaps feeling sorry for me, agreed to have dinner. Seeing only a dirty mug of coffee and a big piece of meat on her plate, she started acting nervous. I tried to calm her by offering more meat. She mentioned something about a forgotten engagement she needed to attend at that moment.

"These are civilized times," a friend advised after. "Girls like things like recipes, marinades, and tenderized meat. As a meat hunter, you need to evolve."

Change scared me. One day you're perfectly content with caribou, coffee, and an outhouse, then you start doing weird things like using marinades and tenderizing meat. Before you know it, you're fretting over which set of floral towels best compliments your bathroom's wallpaper. Yet I couldn't deny how much better tasting and tender meat was when I took a couple extra minutes to cut away the sinew and filament. Soon I was experimenting with marinades and recipes; I embarked on one culinary odyssey after another that all ended happily in my belly.

Having evolved in my meat-hunting ways, I soon became the hit at many dinner parties, except for a couple when I didn't get the memo that most folks at the party would be vegetarians.

"This isn't gamey like venison is supposed to taste. It's delicious! Can I have more?" I heard that enough times to make me wonder if there was some sort of a conspiracy against wild game. Most game will be delicious if a hunter takes the time in the field and the kitchen to treat the meat with respect it deserves. Some instances, such as taking a big buck during the rut or an old mountain goat, warrant burgering and canning most of an animal due to slight gaminess or toughness. Canning is a great way to turn sixty pounds of smelly meat chock-full of hormones into excellent eating. Canning game you forgot from last season is a good way to maximize taste as well as space in your freezer for fresh meat.

All this writing has me drooling. I think I'm going open a can of venison for breakfast burritos and marinate some steaks for dinner. My girlfriend, a vegetarian for years until she met me, is sighing in disbelief.

"I can't believe I'm eating meat for breakfast again and liking it."

"Wait till dinner—the steaks will be even better!" I say as I cut away little bits of sinew and filament, pound each steak with a fork, and put them in a bowl to marinate.

In closing, if any art curators are interested in launching a meat-hunting exhibit, feel free to contact me. I have a few ideas, as well as a couple of noble buddies excited about the potential of modeling for artists. They'll work for a few beers and venison if you prepare it right.

NEVER CRY HALIBUT

WHEN I WAS A KID, I was forced to go fishing in a similar way other youngsters are made to go to church or eat vegetables. There were many types of fish to froth, drag, and otherwise disturb the water after—Dolly Varden, pink, coho, chum, and king salmon, to name a few—but none of them made my imagination run wild like halibut.

"How big can they get?" I'd ask my dad.

"Bigger than me," he'd say. It was mythical to consider there were fish bigger than my dad swimming in the ocean's murk.

Most of the halibut we caught were about the size of Ping-Pong paddles, but knowing there was a chance our bait might find its way into the mouth of monster was enough to make me and my brothers plead to stop trolling for cohos and give a halibut hole a try. I couldn't figure out why Dad often seemed reluctant.

"Halibut! It's a big one!" I would scream a few moments after my lead weight bounced on ocean bottom. Not even Reid, my gullible younger brother, bothered to look over. I'd babble as the giant tried to tear the pole from my hands. If it looked like I might lose the rod, Dad would intervene; otherwise, he'd let me battle it out with what often evolved into something bigger than a halibut could possibly grow.

He'd stare off wistfully as other boats slowly dragged for cohos and wince when fishermen waved their nets in preparation of bringing a fish aboard. Usually after a few minutes of groaning, moaning, and whining, the hook popped free, and I breathed a sigh of relief.

"Probably was a whale. Lucky it got off," I'd say. "Might have killed us if I got it to the surface. And even if it didn't, we'd have to tow it back to the dock, and that would likely mean being attacked by killer whales, sharks, or a giant squid."

"You had the bottom!" my older brother, Luke, yelled. I fought back tears, knowing he was jealous because I had more bites and hookups than he did. Somehow he always managed to catch more fish.

Once, after crying halibut, I was doing battle with a monster that felt as big as the bottom. My pole started hammering down. Dad was watching other boats troll, and my two brothers were staring blandly at the slate-gray oceanscape, ignoring me as I tried to figure out why this fish felt so different from all the other halibut I'd hooked and lost.

"Must have the bottom," I shrugged, trying to free the line. Dad tore the pole from my hands.

"Halibut! It's a big one!" he said, bracing himself as the fish ran and line spun out. Complete pandemonium ensued; I grabbed a gaff and started waving it, nearly impaling a number of family members as I tried to get into position.

"It's going to be a while," he grunted and pushed me out of the way. Fishing teaches kids a lot of things, like how to enjoy nature, how to take pride in bringing home dinner, and most importantly how to curse. Right then and there, the swivel popped, freeing the fish, and the old man gave us a fine lesson on how to talk like a halibut fisherman.

Thinking about it now, I can't recall my dad ever swearing except for when he lost fish. Well, there was the time my mom attacked a full-grown black bear with a broom because it was trying to take a bag of flour from her mudroom pantry. The horrified bear left the flour on the shelf and dashed into the forest. There ought to be a "Forget the Gun and the Dog, Beware of the Woman with a Broom" sign posted on the door of my folk's house. Let that be a warning to any burglars considering raiding my mom's pantry. Though small,

Me, age five, fighting something much bigger and more dangerous than any known fish. (Photo courtesy of Lynnette Dihle)

she's a ball of fury and will attack you.

Through the years, I've become pretty good at dressing and acting like a halibut fisherman. My sweatpants and fleece are usually coated with a mixture of crusty salt and slime. I'm not the best, but I'm fairly decent when it comes to swearing, lying, and telling stories. After all, fishing is mostly about fooling other fisherman that you caught more and bigger fish than they did. I work hard but rarely get much done. One might say I'm the ideal fisherman, except that I lack the ability to catch fish, particularly halibut.

As I grew older and was looking for work, I'd put on a wool sweater, wander the docks, and talk, with a hint of an accent, to commercial fishing captains. One would hire me, thinking they were getting a Norwegian secret weapon as a deckhand. Being of Scandinavian descent and not a good fisherman was nearly unheard of. A day or so later, when we'd be far away from port and the price of diesel didn't warrant a return trip, I would confess to being French, which was a quarter true.

"French! Why, if I would have known!" This would be followed by a long soliloquy cursing baguettes, black turtlenecks, and berets. I would threaten to go on strike, but this only excited my captains further. In time, most began to somewhat affectionately call me Jonah and only shook their heads and grumbled when I made a mistake or the fishing was poor. If they knew I was mostly Scandinavian, my health would have suffered for it.

"You look like a bobblehead. You have to be Norwegian!" one skipper said excitedly after he shook my hand and welcomed me aboard his boat. We were crabbing that summer, and I quickly became adept at birding, telling the captain how to stack pots, and making watercolor paintings of him cursing against beautiful backdrops of mountains and ocean. When he asked for a hand, I would tell him I had an acute shellfish allergy.

"Yeah, sorry, I can't touch crab, but I'm almost done writing a poem about how hard crabbing is. Just give me a sec, and I'll read it to you. By the way, can you make me another cup of coffee? Don't forget the cream and sugar this time. And make sure it's organic."

On a rare day off, I borrowed a skiff and dropped a hook into the shallows near the mouth of a spawning salmon stream. Almost instantly a nice halibut bit, and my pole started hammering. Somehow, after slitting its jugular with a dull pocketknife and letting it bleed out for a few minutes, I managed to get the fifty-pound fish aboard with a broken salmon gaff. It was the biggest halibut I'd seen alive. Now that I was an expert, I started offering advice to anyone who'd listen on how to catch halibut.

"They're in the shallows. Everyone's fishing too deep," I told some seasoned fishermen at the bar in Hoonah.

"In the seventies, I hauled a fish to the surface in Frederick Sound that must have weighed 1,500 pounds, and it just spat the hook," an old man said. He shook his head as if he still couldn't believe what he'd seen.

"When I was a kid, I hooked several that were about that size, maybe even bigger, but they all got away," I said, one-upping him.

I got a job longlining for halibut in Cross Sound with Joe and Sandy Craig on the *Njord* the following spring. The halibut I'd caught the previous summer had tripled in weight and multiplied in quantity. On our first day of pulling sets, I was eager to show off my knowledge and skills.

"Halibut!" I cried in the early gray morning as we bobbed in rough seas. Excited, we all grabbed our gaffs and waited as Joe hauled up the longline with hydraulics.

"Gray cod," he said.

"Halibut!" I cried a few minutes later.

"Rougheye," Joe corrected.

"Halibut!"

"Err...starfish," Sandy said and gave Joe a worried look. When the first halibut came to the surface, I frantically whisked the water with my gaff until you could barely see the fish in all the foam. Joe gaffed it in the head, yanked it over the stern, then dispatched it with a perfectly aimed blow from a lead pipe. I had no money, and they didn't want to pay for a floatplane to take me back to Juneau, so they were stuck with me.

Despite my ineptitude and the fishery's often stressful nature, I learned to love wrestling with halibut and wallowing in their blood and slime. The Fairweather mountains beckoned white through the slate-gray world, but I only had eyes for the ocean. When I thought I saw a halibut coming up on the line, I swallowed my urge to cry out and grunted instead. I popped off wolf eels, seven-foot sleeper sharks, skates, and all sorts of strange benthic creatures from hooks. I learned to decipher species of fish as they rose from the murk with a quick glance. I gently freed octopuses, only to have them wrap their tentacles around me in what seemed like a refusal to return to the ocean.

"Stop hugging that octopus," Joe said, laughing as I tried to convince the creature to let go. When we motored back to their home in Elfin Cove with our day's catch, Sandy and I baited hooks and watched sea birds following schools of bait fish and whales sound. Listening to the ocean, the chug of the diesel engine chug, and Sandy telling stories from her decades of commercial fishing and exploring northern Southeast Alaska, it was a rare afternoon it didn't feel good to be alive.

Toward summer's end, realizing the richness of the experiences they were facilitating for me, I felt I ought to be paying them. Perhaps out of philanthropy, they took me on for the next several seasons until they retired from halibut wrangling.

After that first summer, I never looked at halibut with naiveté and wonder again. I enjoyed longlining but no longer found it that exciting. I pulled flopping monsters over the stern then dispatched, bled, and stashed them before going back to work without another thought.

One afternoon, as we were motoring back to the dock, I was slicing bait and tossing guts to an entourage of sea gulls. Glancing at the boatload of dead halibut, I realized I hadn't cried halibut in years. Several of them weighed well over a hundred, even two hundred pounds, but I felt none of the satisfaction and awe I had as a kid when I reeled in a ten-pounder. Sitting on the kill-box, with the gulls shrieking behind the *Njord*, I remembered being six years old and clutching a rod. My dad had just given me the all-clear, so I opened the reel and listened to the sound of the line spooling out as the lead weight zinged the bait down into the ocean's depths. The weight hit the bottom, and I felt connected to an invisible and mysterious world. A few moments later, at the slightest disturbance, I could no longer contain my excitement and yelled "Halibut!" Now, decades later, I stared out onto the broad expanse of ocean and felt a bit nostalgic. A halibut flopped in its death throes. I tossed a clump of kidney into the screeching flock of birds and went back to work.

FISHEMATICS

I REMEMBER when I began to realize the danger of combining math with fishing, something *Today's Journal of Fishermen's Accounting* calls "fishematics." I'd just exited a floatplane at the Elfin Cove dock and shaken hands with Joe Craig, with whom I'd signed on as a deckhand for the summer.

"If you tell anyone our catch numbers, I'll put you on shore to fend for yourself," he warned half-jokingly as we climbed aboard the *Njord*. I was bad with numbers—which, not long after, I learned made me much more likely to become an expert in fishematics. I'd taken the same math class every year in high school and never passed. My poor teacher had burst into tears several times when trying to convey complicated mathematical formulas like counting to me. I'd grunt, hit my desk with a stone, grab a spawned-out salmon I'd found on my way to school, and offer it to her try to make her feel better.

Naturally, with my dim wits and Joe's good humor, we became great friends. He didn't even get annoyed when he'd ask how many salmon we'd gotten after a pass and I could only shrug if the count exceeded ten. He'd always laugh when he asked me to measure a

A haul of coho salmon waiting to be gutted, gilled, and slushed aboard a power troller in Cross Sound.

halibut and I spread my hands apart however long in estimation. Sometimes, he'd let me out on the shores of Yakobi and Chichagof Islands to run around and play with the local brown bears. I was in heaven. Finally I'd entered a world where math was viewed for what it was: a crime against humanity.

Fishematics were a different beast altogether, though. I couldn't remain under Joe's protection forever. After the season, back in Juneau, I began mixing with certain fishermen who loved talking fishematics. At first I felt like I was listening to a foreign language, but soon I mastered the different theorems, postulates, axioms, and equations. I was overcome with the bubbly feeling of belonging, but

I soon became plagued by philosophical questions. If a fisherman doesn't catch any fish and no one's around to see it, did he really not catch any fish? What is the meaning of fishing? Why are there fish rather than no fish? Do fish shape our nature more than fishing does? What is fishing? What is fish? I tried to use fishematics to solve these problems, but the deeper I delved, the more questions arose. It got so bad that I was on the verge of having a nervous breakdown.

On street corners, in alleyways, and in bars, I frequently found myself locked in fishematical debates over the size and quantity of fish, many of which I'd never even caught.

"I don't like to talk about myself or the fish I've caught," I'd said, squaring off against a crusty old-timer who looked like he'd been fishing for at least eight decades. "But thirty-seven years ago, in Frederick Sound, I caught a 164-pound king."

"That's weird. You don't look a day older than twenty, and I've never heard of a king that big," he said. I wasn't lying outright; I was thinking of the six-inch Dolly a small kid had hooked the previous day. I'd grabbed his rod, shoved him aside, and reeled the fish in. By using the exaggeration theory, one of the more popular fishematical theorems, I was well within the realm of truth. The old man looked off into the distance. His eyes grew misty. In a faraway voice, he said, "Sixty years ago, on the Outer Coast, I caught an eighty-pounder."

"I can one-up that!" I said. "Earlier today I reeled in a ninety-pounder in Auke Bay."

Here I was using the baloney axiom, another fishematic favorite. The old man mumbled something about it being the most beautiful fish he'd ever seen.

Inevitably, like many wayward young fishermen, I got swept away and soon cared more about fishematics than fishing. In boats, on docks, and in bars, sometimes a whisper, sometimes a scream, fishematics followed me. I sank so low that a three-inch Dolly Varden caught on Saturday would grow into a twenty-five-pound king salmon by Monday. The one strike I had during a day of trolling would turn into the limit of cohos when a friend phoned and asked how the fishing was. When I lost hook, flasher, and sinker after snagging the bottom, I'd blame it on the accursed white whale that had been following me ever since I began my career as a fisherman.

All of this I fishematically justified.

Fishematics did get me out of a bind once, though. A Fish and Game technician measuring a king told me it was twenty-seven and three-quarters inches long. The legal length was twenty-eight inches. I evoked the shrinkage equation to argue against a citation.

"When a fish gets cold, it loses a few inches," I said. "What the... someone's breaking into your truck!" While the technician frantically looked the other way, I grasped the tail and head and stretched out the fish the best I could. My fishematical argument was so tight he let me slide without measuring the fish again.

By the following spring, when I boarded a floatplane to Elfin Cove, I was a shaking, babbling, drooling mess. Gray, undulating ocean and mist-clad islands stretched to the distant horizons. Seeing Joe and his wife Sandy set my soul at ease, and soon I fell into a therapeutic routine. Out on the ocean, amidst the whales and mountains, I gradually remembered the person I was before fishematics hijacked my life. With each real fish landed, my illusions grew weaker. On occasion when our work was done, I'd sit atop a rock high above the crashing surf and ponder the sound of one hand fishing. After a couple of weeks, enough time to really let the halibut slime and blood soak in, I forgot fishematical questions all together.

HIGH COUNTRY BLACKTAILS OF ADMIRALTY

DURING THE SUMMER OF 2015, my little brother, Reid, was faced with a tough decision. His first child was due to be born around August 1, which also happened to be opening day for Sitka blacktail deer. This meant he was going to have to be real tricky and risk his marriage if he wanted to get out after a buck. I suggested sneaking into the mountains for a morning hunt and returning in time to feed his newborn raw deer heart. Reid was philosophical, even superstitious, about the predicament.

"It will be a boy. I'll name him Ruger Olaf Dihle, and he will become the greatest hunter ever," he said. The summer passed quickly, and his wife Meghan's belly plumped up like a blueberry.

Our older brother, Luke, had been dreaming of little other than opening day since he'd finished his hunting season the previous winter. He's kind of the John Lennon of meat hunters, the sort of guy who dreams big, needs two giant freezers, and has a fan base of young girls (his three daughters). His girls are more efficient at butchering and processing fish and game than the majority of outdoorsmen, including me. It's always a little embarrassing when a seven-year-old shows you up filleting a salmon on the docks.

Generally speaking, Luke can talk Reid into doing anything when it comes to hunting. For example, let's say there's a mountain goat three mountains over, a blizzard coming, and little chance of my brothers finding their way back to the tent for several days if they go. Throw in a sexually frustrated Sasquatch, a few KGB hit men, and a series of vertical cliffs that would liquefy the bowels of most professional mountaineers. Luke would still want to make the stalk. With a few grunts, he'd convince Reid. I'd sit at the tent drinking whiskey, eating Cheez-Its, and getting weird. So it was a bit of a disturbing surprise when Reid decided not to join us on the annual August 1 foray. Whatever happened to putting family first?

Luke is obsessed with mountain goats; it's his favorite species to hunt. It's gotten so bad that often when I walk into his house, he and his wife Trish are dressed up like goats and butting heads. For years he's wanted to pull a doubleheader, first making a goat hunt on the mainland south of Juneau. Afterward, if we had luck, he wanted to put the meat in a tote of ice on his boat and jaunt up a mountain on Admiralty Island for Sitka blacktails. I, as the token fat guy on our hunts, am horrified and exhausted just thinking about this. Under the guise of being a good brother, this particular year I suggested we do one hunt or the other and then try to be back in town for the birth of Reid and Meghan's baby. I was, after all, Meghan's substitute birthing coach. I took the job very seriously and had stocked up on forties of Steel Reserve, barf bags, a mixed CD of meditation music, and a variety of Little Debbie tasty snacks to make the whole process more enjoyable for me. So if the weather was good, we'd climb high and try for goats. If the weather was marginal, we'd clamber up a smaller mountain and go after deer. If we were lucky, the baby would be late, and we'd make it back in time to pretend we were good uncles.

On July 31, after a cup of coffee, I shouldered my pack and walked down to the South Douglas boat launch to meet Luke. Meghan's contractions were becoming more regular. I had a suspicion that it would not be long; nonetheless, we tore off onto a flat ocean. We were cowboys, maybe even desperadoes, the sort of men who drink kale smoothies and occasionally leave the toilet seat up to spite our ladies. We kept a sharp lookout in the fog and steady rain as there are plenty of things like icebergs, deadheads, rocks, whales, and other boats to run into in Stephens Passage. Humpback whales appeared for a few moments like giant gray ghosts before sounding back into the depths. Loons, surf scoters, and harlequin ducks skimmed over the ocean and then conglomerated in large, raucous rafts. Salmon on their way to spawn in streams and rivers leapt constantly into the air. Gradually the fog began to lift, revealing the rainforest mountains of Admiralty Island.

"Going after a goat would be iffy," I said, staring up at heavy clouds clinging to the mountains on the mainland. Rain drummed the canvas top of Luke's skiff.

"Yeah, we might just be sitting in the clouds for days. You want to give Admiralty a try?" Luke asked.

While I enjoy hunting and eating those white mountain monarchs, I'd rather chase deer. An August buck, if the meat is properly cared for, is delectable. I'd been drooling for a month or more just thinking about the first venison of the year. I nodded, and we slowly putted past a reef and entered a large bay. Inquisitive harbor seals circled the boat as Luke anchored. I studied brown bear, deer, mink, and otter tracks crisscrossing the tidal flats. The easiest place to hang and stash our gear was in a small stand of spruce trees near a salmon stream. We hoisted our deflated raft as high as we could above a couple of well-used bear beds. After pissing around the tree in hopes of discouraging any bruins from doing too thorough a job investigating, we hiked along bear trails through a series of meadows.

Admiralty Island is the paradigm of Southeast Alaskan wilderness. Its true name is Kootznoowoo, which in Tlingit means something like "Fortress of the Brown Bear." The Russians called it Fear Island. A hundred miles long by about twenty-five miles wide, many believe it has the densest population of brown bears in the world, at one per square mile. Annually, around fifty bears are killed on the island by sports hunters. The hunters target big males, which isn't thought to negatively affect the population. Males kill cubs and subadults to eat and bring females into estrus, so some say it may even help. I'm hesitant to drink that Kool-Aid but will vouch that there definitely appears to be no shortage of bears on the island. Many people are surprised to learn that Admiralty has only one documented case of a bear killing a person, a timber cruiser in

Eliza Harbor in 1929, after he startled and shot the bear.

Nonetheless, Luke and I hollered as we waded through thick brush towards a steep ridge. The blueberries and huckleberries were so thick we kept getting distracted from hiking. Soon, we both had purple mouths. Zigzagging up game trails and through devil's club, we eventually crested the ridge and found a nice critter trail to follow.

In the evening, we broke out of tree line and into the disorienting swirl of clouds. Wandering around in the fog on Admiralty is always a little unnerving. It's easy to get turned around, and there's always the possibility of stepping on a bear—an exciting but rarely enjoyable phenomenon that often ends with both bear and human unexpectedly having diarrhea. One bear I ran into crapped so much as it ran away I couldn't help but think the words *fecal propulsion*. Personally, I prefer crapping my pants privately. Or in the company of my gal, MC. For some strange reason, it brings her no end of joy. She lights up whenever she tells another "And then Bjorn pooped his pants" story at the wine tasting and etiquette parties we frequently attend.

Luke and I bumbled into a doe and then a small spike-fork that stared at us with tragic innocence just twenty yards away.

"Maybe we should set up camp here before we spook the rest of the area," Luke suggested.

While eating dinner, we watched the small buck and a couple of does come in and out of view as the wind swirled sheets of mist. It was well after dark when I took our food a short ways from camp to hang in a mountain hemlock tree. I was pissing around the area when I heard Luke scream, "No! No! This can't be happening!" If he was being mauled by a bear, his aggressor was the quiet type. Maybe a mute bear. Or perhaps it was the KGB or the IRS. I knew those lowlifes would eventually catch up with me. I hustled back to find Luke holding a flashing, beeping gadget that looked like it was thinking about blowing up.

"What the heck?" I asked.

"I accidentally hit the rescue button on my new inReach tracker!" he yelled.

I bellowed with laughter as he cursed and hammered the touch screen. What a funny story! I could tease him forever about this! I could just see the headlines in the newspaper now: "Deer hunter rescued after electronic accident." Suddenly I realized I was with Luke and would suffer the same sort of defamation. Reid would tease us forever about this. We put our heads together and tried to figure out how to turn the thing off. Nothing seemed to work. Soon we were both screaming.

"I'm going to throw it off a cliff!" I yelled. "No, wait! I'm going to shoot it!"

A half hour of horror later, both of us were still hyperventilating, but we'd finally figured out how to turn the cursed thing off and send a message asking not to be rescued. We rolled into our sleeping bags a bit emotionally exhausted but looking forward to first light.

The bowl we camped next to was devoid of deer in the morning, likely a result of our theatrical performance the night before. Glassing with our rifle scopes, we slowly clambered up the ridge and into the clouds. In the far distance, we made out three bucks—all looked like nice fork-horns and frying-pan trophies. Southeast Alaska's deer are a smaller subspecies of blacktails, whose ancestors wandered up the northwest coast to Southeast Alaska around ten thousand or so years ago when massive glaciers began to melt. They intrepidly made miles-wide ocean crossings and colonized virtually every island. Through time, they grew stockier and smaller, and became more accustomed to the rain and darkness. When heavy snows came, most starved to death or died from exposure. Even today, populations vary greatly depending on the winters. Fish and Game estimates there are roughly 200,000 blacktails in Southeast— give or take quite a few, depending on the winter—with hunters annually harvesting around 12,300. Some hunters prefer to go after early season bucks in the high country; others like to wait for the late season when snows push them down.

The clouds broke, revealing a beautiful expanse of mountains and ocean. It was a clear reminder of why I love hunting the early season the best. We crept from rock to boulder and spotted another three deer below in a valley some five hundred yards away. One was a decent fork, but there was no way to continue without being seen. Luke, wanting a bigger buck, suggested hiking on and risking spooking the area. I'd never passed on shooting a fork-horn and wasn't about to start, even if there were bigger bucks around. When the clouds rolled back in and shrouded us, we made a rapid descent into a gorge. I climbed out and spied the buck, but it was bit far for a shot, and I didn't have a good rest. Soon mist swirled back in, and I crawled another hundred yards to the edge of the valley. I bundled up my jacket, chambered a round, and waited. Minutes later, as the clouds began to thin, I made out the shape of deer moving below. Gradually, the buck's antlers appeared out of the gray. I waited until he turned to the side and fired; he fell over and lay still.

"Well," Luke said, as the clouds rolled back in. "I think I'll roll on and try to find that four-by-four."

We have a long-standing joke about a mythical four-by-four buck. Reid once told Luke he'd retire from hunting if Luke ever shot one. Two years prior, I was standing with Luke when a true monarch popped its head up at dusk just twenty yards away. I'd just taken a fat fork-horn and was about to climb down a steep slope to gut it and splay it open to cool overnight. Well, that moose of a deer looked up, and Luke, without a moment's hesitation, fired. It tumbled down a slope. After I'd taken care of my deer, I turned on my headlamp and climbed over and found Luke reassembling a giant, broken set of antlers.

"It was at least a four-by-four," he said, shrugging.

Back on Admiralty, I took every ounce of usable meat off the buck and kept the ribs intact for Luke's three daughters to gnaw on. For years their favorite meal was deer ribs. Recently they were becoming more sophisticated.

It was a long, slow hike back to the crest of the ridge. Rain and wind buffeted me as I sat above camp looking out on the ocean. Luke emerged from the swirling clouds, I shouldered my pack, we hiked down to the tent, and he told me about his hunt.

He'd been skirting along the ridge, slowly approaching the three bucks we'd seen earlier, when a bowl full of deer came into view. Right off the bat, he noticed three big guys, including a three-by-four bedded down. He crawled and snuck from bush to bush until he was almost within range, which for him can be well over three hundred yards. He looked to his right and saw two bucks watching and acting like they might spook. If this were to happen, all the deer

Reid and Luke with a nice Sitka blacktail in the high country of Admiralty Island. (Photo courtesy of Luke Dihle)

in the bowl would likely run off. He had a good rest, so he shot the larger of the bucks. Luke then rose to his full height and was greeted with a dozen sets of eyes and antlers. The mountain was so remote that they didn't spook while he walked over to begin working on the downed buck.

We broke camp and began the long slog to the ocean. In the late evening, an hour or so before sunset, we made it to the salmon stream. As we inflated the raft and loaded up our gear, the sound of galloping came echoing down the stream. A bear, preoccupied with the salmon it was chasing, was running at us.

"Hey!" I yelled. The horrified bear looked up and peeled out of the creek and into the safety of the forest.

Aboard Luke's skiff, we shared a drink with the bugs. Well, we sipped Rainiers while they drank our blood. A sow and her cub walked along the shore until they disappeared into the gloom. A few deer came out on the tidal flat; we checked for antlers and teased each other about hiking to the top of the mountain when there were deer to shoot on the beach. It was too late to make it back to Juneau, so we elected to spread our sleeping bags out and wake up early to do a little halibut fishing before heading home.

"More deer," I said, gesturing at the beach as we motored up the bay. Luke shook his head. We dropped our lines, which were baited with chunks of a humpy we'd caught that morning off a point. A lot of the time, halibut fishing around Juneau can be slow and unproductive, but that day we had hits almost as soon as our leads hit the bottom. Within an hour, we had four twenty-five-pounders, the size that makes for some of the best eating. For the first time in several days, the sun burned through the clouds, and we had breathtaking vistas on the ride back to Juneau. Humpback whales were everywhere, and at one point, a pod of thirty or so killer whales swam past. Some of the more playful and inquisitive ones came for a closer look when Luke put the boat in neutral.

We were eager for news on Reid and Meghan, and we soon found out the baby was indeed born on August 1. Her name was Wren Meadows Dihle; after a rough start in this world, she was doing well. I processed the fish as fast as I could, cleaned up the ribs for my nieces, and headed over with MC to Reid and Meghan's home. Luke's girls were sitting outside holding their cousin. Braith, seven years old, showed me how to hold Wren.

"Why didn't you name her Ruger Olaf?" I asked Reid.

"Don't worry, she'll still become the greatest hunter ever," my little brother said as he proudly looked at his little girl.

Dear Nutrition.gov,

Please Sponsor My Alaskan Diet Plan

Today, I'm offering you the chance to sponsor the new and exciting Alaskan Diet Plan (ADP). Before I delve too deeply into the ins and outs of ADP, let me tell you a little about myself and how I came up with this awesome program.

My spiritual journey to become skinny and attractive began on the set of the movie *Magic Mike*. There'd been a posting that the production was looking for a hot, young, uninhibited man to fetch coffee and clean Porta Potties (apparently there were a lot of splash issues going on). I auditioned for the job, figuring I'd soon become best friends with Channing Tatum and Matthew McConaughey and inevitably become ridiculously good looking. To my despair, the producer told me I looked like a cross between Samwise Gamgee from *The Lord of the Rings* and Bigfoot, and that I had no future in Hollywood.

Crushed, I took to wandering the hinterlands much like the character Tristan—played by Brad Pitt—in the movie *Legends of the Fall*. I had all sorts of crazy adventures, but none are worth relating—no one would care. I wasn't skinny and attractive in those days.

I tried every diet and fitness plan, beginning with the more popular trends and devolving into more obscure practices. I enjoyed some more than others, but nothing worked. The marsupial diet was kind of cool; I'd never eaten koala bear meat before. The tiger blood juicing diet led to some interesting social interchanges and a tragic encounter with a car full of a family that looked like they'd just gotten out of church that I kind of attacked after one intense juicing session. Oh, the underwater lunar eclipse yoga camp was cool, but something horrible happened to many of the practitioners involving downward dog pose and a school of poisonous jellyfish.

I thought a lot about things during this period. For a little while, I even wondered if beauty might be more than skin deep, if there might be more to life than looking like a model. I know you're laughing, but please remember it was a very confusing time for me.

Plagued by harpies of doubt, I thought I'd never look like Channing, Matthew, or Brad—until out of the blue, the wildest idea occurred to me. Maybe my epic quest to become skinny and beautiful, a journey that took me to all four corners of the earth and into the bowels of Mordor and out the urethra of Hollywood, was all unnecessary. Maybe the remedy was looking me right in the face all that time. I stared back, and what did I see? Alaska. Spell it backwards: Aksala, which I'm pretty sure in Greek, Latin, or some other weird language means "the skinny land."

Now, here's where things get really exciting! The Alaskan Diet Plan was founded on the crazy belief that if you wander around in the woods, tundra, and mountains long enough and without sufficient food, you'll lose weight. With this assumption, I asked my friend Ben if he wanted to join me on a pilot test. Without hesitation, he was in.

We picked a walk from Arctic Village to Kaktovik, a south-to-north traverse of the Arctic National Wildlife Refuge (ANWR). Some say the refuge is the last great wilderness in North America and needs to be protected from drilling for oil. Proponents of development claim drilling would be good for the economy and cut down on our dependency on foreign petroleum. I say ANWR's greatest importance is that it offers every one of us the chance to become skinny and attractive through the ADP. It's my deepest belief that one day the two anachronisms will become conjoined. Just imagine, ANWRADP!

ADP is so simple and easy, it's genius. Go to a remote place, shoulder a heavy pack, and start walking. Try to quit ADP, and you either die or have to call for a very expensive rescue. If you're really desperate, amp it up and get giardia or eat a brown bear's tapeworm. You see how it works.

Another amazing benefit of the ADP is that walking hundreds of miles with a heavy backpack is great for chafing—err, I mean, exfoliating. The sun and the wind give you a wonderful face tan. All those freezing cold rivers you ford have similar effects to going to the most exclusive spas. Bushwhacking is kind of like taking a mud bath and getting a Thai massage at the same time. Running out of food and starving is a great way to detox. The stress from getting lost and aggressive encounters with grizzly and polar bears does wonders for culling your appetite. I mean, are you really going to be thinking about eating when something is thinking about eating you?

As you can see, ADP is foolproof. I look forward to working with you, but you must act fast. I'm querying a number of other agencies, nonprofits, and individuals for sponsorship.

Stay forever skinny,
Bjorn Dihle

Me during a 400-mile ski across the eastern Brooks Range to try to lose fifteen pounds and get a nice face and hand tan. (Photo courtesy of Ben Crozier)

GOAT OBSESSION

OBSESSION COMES in many forms—money, power, sex, and acclaim, to name a few—and has led to the ruination of many people. In northern Southeast Alaska, obsessions often manifest in the form of compulsive fishing and hunting. For my younger brother, Reid, it's the dream of catching a giant halibut. For me, it's wandering around in the woods hoping that something big and hairy will jump out and make me feel something. For my older brother, Luke, it's hunting the sage-like, white, hairy, and horned beast that lives in rugged mountains, known to the world as the mountain goat.

In late winter of 2012, as the snow amassed in valleys and storms tore at the mountains of northern Southeast Alaska, I found myself fantasizing about adventures elsewhere. The phone rang, flashing a number with an area code from somewhere down south.

"Hello, this is Joe Fuchochewo," a man said with a nasal twang. "Am I talking to Bee-jorn Die-gila?"

"Err...yeah."

"Hello, Bjorn! I just won the lottery! I drew one of the two mountain goat tags for the hunt north of Juneau!" Joe yelled. "You're a guide, right? I read about you in *Hunt Alaska Magazine*. Great stuff, though your older brother sounds like a real a-hole! I want you to be my guide!"

"I'm sorry, but I don't have a guide license," I said after the man got done yelling. I thought I heard laughing in the background. My older brother, Luke, wanted that once-in-a-lifetime tag something fierce. He'd been at the Seattle Children's Hospital coping with an illness in his family for the last few months. He would be upset to find out some joker drew his dream tag then had the nerve to ask me to guide him illegally.

"I heard you have a good reputation. I want you to be my guide," Joe said.

"Ah, I guide stuff like bear viewing, kayak trips, and film crews," I said. Now I was sure I heard a woman laughing.

"Kayak? What's a kayak? Whoopee! Let's go mountain goat hunting!"

"I have a number of friends who are hunting guides. They might be able to help you," I said and began listing names and numbers. Laughter echoed in the background.

"Luke?" I asked. "Is that you?"

"Yeah," he said. "I got the mountain goat tag. What are you doing next October?"

"Hunting with you, I guess," I said, chuckling.

In the ensuing months, Luke's goat obsession got so bad that Reid and I wondered if we should stage an intervention. Walking into his house, you felt like you were entering some sort of pagan ritual with all the horns, antlers, and hides he had everywhere. There were rumors he was sleep-hunting and having "goat terrors." One day I confronted him on his obsession.

"There are other things in life, you know, besides hunting mountain goats," I said. "Why are you so obsessed?"

"I have no poetic explanation," Luke said. "Goats are the toughest, most majestic animal. They live in country where nothing else lives. I love hunting deer, caribou, and sheep, but there's nothing like being in goat country."

I had to agree with him there. I'd been wandering goat country since I was fifteen and still felt lucky whenever I was in their mountains. They're the only member of the goat-antelope family to be found in North America. They mature much more slowly than most other ungulates, reaching their breeding age at around five years old. Nannies have one kid annually until they're around eight years old, meaning they have the slowest and shortest reproductive lives of all Alaskan ungulates. The Alaska Department of Fish and Game encourages hunters to harvest male goats. A guide or next of kin is required by law to accompany out-of-state hunters, mostly because mountain goats are the most dangerous animal to hunt in Alaska.

During the summer, Luke would go and scout the ridges and mountains. Scouting in Southeast Alaska can be complicated by the fact we have a lot of what we call "liquid sunshine." Sometimes an entire month will pass without the sun breaking through the clouds, something a lot of us are proud of. For Luke, the rain and the clouds meant he rarely had a chance to glass the terrain. After each scouting mission, he'd return home a bit disappointed, saying he saw plenty of wolf sign but no goats. Finally on a nasty day in September, just two weeks before goat season opened, during a break in the storm, he spied a massive billy on a desolate mountain surrounded by glacier. His goat terrors subsided a bit, but his erratic behavior continued.

Two weeks later, I tried to keep pace with him and Reid as we hiked under dripping boughs, through muck, and into a sickly forest. We climbed into the foggy subalpine and bumped into a flock of sooty grouse clucking nervously. Hoping for a delicious dinner, I hurled my ice ax at a large rooster and missed by about ten feet, so far that the bird didn't even move.

"Just trying to teach them people aren't safe," I said as my brothers laughed. They proceeded to make fun of me until we found a suitable site for a base camp next to a kettle pond. We pitched tents, stashed extra gear, and then pushed on against the wind, rain, and snow. We climbed blindly into the precipitous world of the mountain goat. Wolf scat, partly digested bones, and goat poop lay in piles every so often. Before long, the wind tore a hole in the clouds, revealing a half dozen goats on surrounding mountains. Luke set up his spotting scope, and after ten minutes of studying and deliberating, we agreed they all looked like nannies and young. Though it was legal to take a nanny, Luke would only shoot a billy.

The ridge narrowed into a knife blade before horseshoeing

A young male mountain goat superimposed against a glacier.

around to the edge of a glacier. A flock of thirty rock ptarmigan flew from the ridge and landed on a patch of snow in the lee of the wind. Hoping the weather would clear enough to glass the surrounding mountains, we hunkered behind boulders above the glacier and waited. This was the area where Luke had seen the big billy two weeks prior. The fog rose above the valley to the south, revealing a goat bedded down on a steep slope. We were unsure of its sex, but with daylight slowly running out, we decided to make a stalk. We snuck by croaking ptarmigan using a series of ravines for cover and crawled within 150 yards of the animal. My first guess was female. Luke set up the spotting scope and verified it was a nanny. We crawled away, and the goat didn't even stir from its bed. The wind died and the clouds lifted, revealing fresh snow on black and jagged mountains. The setting sun illuminated the red, green, and yellow of the alpine in soft light.

"There's a wolf or a wolverine up there," Luke said, gesturing up at a high ridge. The animal, a round and light-colored speck, was superimposed against a glacier and a black mountain. Reid and I guessed it was probably a wolverine as Luke set up his spotting scope. "It's a glacier bear!"

Sure enough, the grayish-blue animal was a bear. We took turns watching it graze on the last of the year's low-bush blueberries and crowberries. Darkness caught us climbing a steep slope covered in rotten deer lettuce. We crested a ridge and looked out on the silhouettes of the Chilkat Range across Lynn Canal as the last bit of red dissipated into black. We strapped on our headlamps, picked our way down a wolf and mountain goat trail, and found camp forty-five minutes later. Soon after, Luke cooked up a delicious dinner of hot dogs and couscous. Somewhere in the darkness, amidst the forest of bull pines and mountain hemlocks, I thought I heard a grouse clucking happily.

"Let's go, it's clear," Luke said in the morning as I worked on my third mug of coffee.

"What about sun salutations?" I asked. Luke growled. "But I still haven't had my thirty-minute bowel movement." Tossing coffee into the bushes, I chased after my brothers as the dawn slowly illuminated an expanse of mountains, forest, and ocean. Feeling like my heart was about to explode, I tried to play head games with Luke to slow him down.

"Is that a goat?" I asked between breaths, gesturing at a distant white rock. This earned me about a five-second break, time enough for Luke to snort a few times in disgust. I finally convinced him to stop running with the excuse that we needed to better glass the surrounding ridges and slopes. We soon spotted two massive goats resting on a bench surrounded by what looked like near-vertical cliffs. Another goat, a nanny, walked along the valley below. The terrain was heinously steep, but we had packed ice axes, crampons, and a hundred feet of rope. We backtracked and descended a mountain until we came to a series of cliffs. Strapping on crampons, we took extra care as we traversed the mountainside.

"Lord, that looks steep," I said as we peered above a cliff at the two goats.

"Maybe if we descend out of view, we can follow a ravine up and get within range. The cliff they're on looks impossible to climb though," Luke whispered. We crawled out of sight and climbed down to a bench covered in mountain hemlock trees. We crawled toward the lip of the ravine until we ran out of cover.

"They'll see us for sure," I said.

A few moments later, Luke hissed with excitement. Bedded about five hundred yards away, with only its head visible, was a goat. After studying it through the spotting scope for a few minutes, Luke looked at us with big eyes.

"I think it's a billy. Take a look."

I studied the animal carefully, waiting for it to offer a side profile. Sure enough, its horns had wide bases and a subtle curve.

"It's a billy. It doesn't look nearly as big as the boys up on the cliffs, but it's mature. What do you think?" I asked Luke. He made a strange moaning sound then rapidly belly crawled in the goat's direction, leaving Reid and me panting and unable to keep up. If you've ever seen the movie *The Last of the Mohicans*, you may remember the opening scene of Hawkeye and Uncas chasing down an elk. That's Luke toward the end of a stalk, except that he generally keeps his shirt on. By the time we reached Luke, he was within 220 yards and already had a rest. At the shot, the billy rose into a majestic pose before tumbling into a ravine. The goat was nine or ten years old, toward the end of its years, and had a rotting back hoof. Its horns measured nine and three-quarters inches, despite their broken tips. Luke knelt and put his hand on the animal.

"Thank you, goat; thank you, God," he said.

Carrying heavy packs—the goat would yield more than 110 pounds of delicious meat—to camp, we jumped what looked like a small wolf in the brush. We climbed up and down ravines and across steep slippery slopes until we made it back to our tents in the evening. While eating heart pasta, we stared at rugged mountains and hanging glaciers, and listened to the deep quiet of goat country. None of us were in a rush to get home.

FORTYMILE CARIBOU

IN AUGUST OF 2012, I found myself in the middle of an Alaskan soap opera.

"I can't get time off," my little brother and Dad said in unison. These horrible five words that have haunted history since the Industrial Age knocked the wind out of my older brother, Luke.

"Looks like the caribou hunt's a no-go then," he said.

"I can still come," I piped in. Steely eyed, he said nothing and went back to stacking a mountain of firewood in his driveway. I'd earlier suggested the possibility of my girlfriend, MC, accompanying us on the hunt. My brothers stared at me at first in amusement and then in growing irritation.

"We're not progressive. A woman along? Part of the reason we go hunting is to get away from them. Are you trying to ruin something that's sacred?"

I went home feeling I had betrayed my family. A week later, my phone rang.

"I'm still going even if Reid and Dad can't," my brother said. Then he offered somewhat begrudgingly, "You can come if you want. Fish and Game made an aerial survey, and it sounds like there are virtually no caribou off the Taylor Highway."

"Great! I'll tell MC you're excited for her to come!"

A week later, after taking a ferry from Juneau to Haines, we drove north. Things weren't too different; we still talked incessantly about hunting and wildlife and often broke wind. MC, not always knowing the ins and outs of the conversation, could at least make silent yet deadly contributions to the long ride. Willows and aspens were yellowing with the onset of fall. Evening sunbeams shone wildly across the blue expanse of Kluane Lake and the surrounding rugged, shale-covered mountains.

The following day, we drove along the Taylor Highway, through taiga and canyons, to one of the areas reserved for nonmotorized hunters. A harsh northerly blew as we trudged through a cemetery of charcoaled logs and lifeless, standing black spruce. Long alpine ridges covered in tussocks, dwarf willows, and rock rose out of the dead forest. No tents were in view, a sure sign folks had heard Fish and Game's report and were seeking other ways to fill their freezers. Snow on higher ridges and the frigid wind made me worry about MC. She wasn't nearly as good at being hypothermic as me or Luke. I looked back. Snot was streaming down her pink chin, and she smiled. A few old caribou tracks indented the mud on ancient game trails. Five hours later, we pitched a base camp on a small bench and enjoyed a hot dinner as the setting sun illuminated cotton grass and the ghostly expanse of tundra. The moon, pale and nearly full, rose above a ridge lit up with alpenglow.

"I'm impressed with her," Luke said as MC moved off toward the tents. "Most men would have had a hard time hiking in today, but she kept up fine. I'm even a little tired. Looks like Fish and Game weren't kidding—I didn't even see a fresh caribou track."

The morning dawned crisp and clear; as I expected, Luke had torn away from camp in the darkness. After hot mugs of black tea, MC and I climbed the rocky ridge behind camp.

"It's so beautiful here. So much space," she whispered as I slowly glassed every nook and cranny.

"Not a breath of boo," I whispered back, and we continued down the ridge, surprising a nearly black cross fox. The little fellow sprinted fifty yards then stopped and watched us for a few moments

MC and a caribou antler shed in the mountains above the Yukon River.

before dropping out of sight. At every likely vantage point, we sought out a boulder for a windbreak then glassed the surrounding valleys. A good six miles from camp, we spied Luke at the top of a high peak. We followed a game trail up a steep scree slope, the wind knocking us off balance at times.

"Anything?" Luke asked.

"Nothing. Just a cross fox. You?"

"Nope. Just a wolf across a valley."

Mountains, stirring and lonesome, stretched in all directions. We sat on the summit as long as we could before the waning hours and frigid temperatures forced us back to camp.

The following day, after exploring and glassing from another ridge system, MC and I sat in the twilight waiting expectantly for Luke to return. In near darkness, his form metamorphosed out of a field of tussocks. He was walking at his usual quick gait, but I could tell he was tired. He dropped his pack heavily to the ground as I tended the camp stove to reheat dinner.

"I smell caribou," I said. He filled us in on the day's advents. In the late afternoon, he'd noticed three caribou far off, down in a valley. Even though they appeared to be cows and it was late, he snuck down for a closer look. At three hundred yards, a cow noticed him; he lay motionless next to a scrub spruce as she grew more nervous. Another caribou stepped out, and Luke, seeing its larger size and the difference in its antler formation, judged it to be a three-year-old bull. A much better shot than me, he filled his tag without crawling another yard. On his way back to camp, a mile or so away, he collapsed atop a tussock to rest, and a young bull caribou trotted by within forty yards.

I woke in the predawn gloom hoping to spend the first half of the day helping Luke get his caribou back to camp and the second half glassing with MC. I shook his tent harder and harder, trying to rouse him. His ability to sleep soundly, even in country loaded with grizzlies, has always impressed me. As I considered making a low moan and a grunt, a lone bull came running across the tundra a half mile away.

"Big bull! I'm going to try to cut him off!" I hissed. Luke was immediately wide awake. I crawled into the brush and sprinted over tussocks, erupting a flock of willow ptarmigan, to a small knoll. Lying behind brush, the hammering of my heart gradually subsided as minutes passed. I stuck my head up and searched the empty tundra, but the caribou was gone.

Later, when Luke and I were nearing the spot where he had shot his caribou, he noticed some specks moving high on a mountain.

"Six caribou. I know we're far away, but we've still got a few days to get meat back," he said, looking through his scope.

"You know, we're probably the only fools in Alaska willing to hike a caribou thirteen miles to the road," I said.

"Yeah, if anyone ever found out, they'd laugh at us. Not noticing any definite bulls. Want to try to cut them off? Could be a young bull in there."

"The smaller, the better," I said, thinking how painful the pack out would be. We hustled across the mountainside to a ravine where the caribou might funnel down. A stream rushed over rocks and braided into a valley ablaze with red lichens and yellow willows. We waited a half hour before deciding they'd chosen a different route.

Later, MC and I sat high on a mountain watching the light play across the lonely mountains, hills, and valleys.

"I love this," she said, gesturing out across the land. "I don't really care if we get a caribou, though it would be nice to have the meat."

"Well, we got one more day to really hunt," I said as we began hiking back to camp.

We woke in darkness, broke chunks of ice into a cook pot, and soon filled our mugs with steaming black tea. The sun slowly illuminated frozen tussocks as we trekked out of camp. A dark gray wolf came streaking across a flat expanse of tundra. It veered off to a distance of four hundred yards then paused to stare.

"Maybe a good sign for today," MC said, smiling. The wolf disappeared toward Luke, who was hauling a load of meat back to the truck.

Around two o'clock, as storm clouds were slowly blotting out the horizon, I noticed a few caribou three-quarters of a mile away.

"Some caribou down there," I said, and MC perked up. "One looks like it might be a bull. Kind of late, and we're twelve miles from the road. What do you want to do?"

"Let's go for it!" she hissed, a far cry from the vegetarian I'd met a couple of years ago.

Choosing a route that kept us out of view, we crept across the scree-covered mountainside as fast and quietly as we could. We were belly crawling when the first caribou, a mature cow, appeared below at two hundred yards. A smaller caribou followed, then one that was nearly twice the size. Maybe a three-year-old bull, but I wasn't taking any chances. MC, panting, her eyes huge, let out a deep exhale and looked at me wildly after the caribou moved out of view. I was a little flustered that such a kind, sweet woman could so quickly morph into a ravenous predator. We belly crawled for a few minutes to intercept the three. The two cows trotted into view at about a hundred yards, followed by the bigger caribou. Clearly seeing evidence of sex, I slowly put a bullet into the chamber then looked over at MC.

"Do you want me to take him?" I whispered, thinking about how hard the pack out was going to be. She nodded; I calmed my breath and steadied my aim. The bull fell heavily to the earth, his legs gently kicking a few times. Kneeling over him, MC felt the warmth of his body. The two cows stood watching from a few hundred yards away.

Getting ready to hike out the next day, Luke stole one of my game bags of meat and gave me a bag, comparable in weight, filled with meat from his caribou.

"I don't want you to be able to say you hauled your whole caribou by yourself," he said. MC had most of the communal camping gear in her backpack.

"You want MC to take any more of your stuff? She can carry your pack if you get tired," I teased as we hiked down through the brush.

"Look, I'm not that bad. I'm intimidated by women versus thinking men are tougher. I know enough to know we're the weaker sex," he said and then streaked ahead with his hundred-plus-pound pack.

I thanked the country and the caribou for what they had given and slowly followed.

A BLOODY BUSINESS
BUT A GOOD LIFE

IT WAS STILL DARK when we hauled anchor and began motoring from a protected cove on Yakobi Island into the big ocean. The chugging of the *Njord's* diesel engine was lost in the thunder of waves breaking against pinnacles of rock. In a few minutes, we would be plowing through seven-foot waves, lines would be zipping, and hooks would be flying. My guts twisted, and bile rose in my throat. I was a greenhorn deckhanding the big July king salmon troll opener on the tempestuous outer coast of Southeast Alaska. Even more nerve-wracking, I was fishing for Joe Craig, a man many of the Elfin Cove trolling fleet deemed one of the best king salmon trollers around. We bobbed out of the cove and were engulfed in a roller coaster of waves and twenty-five-mile-per-hour winds. Joe came out of the cabin, gave me a look letting me know how worthless I was, and swaggered back to the cockpit where I waited.

"Now! Drop your float first!" he barked. Using a gurdy, we each dropped a fifty-pound lead cannon ball attached to trolling line into the frothing sea. I began manically clipping spreads—a flasher attached to a hoochie or a spoon and evenly placed onto the line—as the cannon ball zipped downwards. Sometimes I panicked and threw the spreads unattached into the water. I'd later blame pesky sea lions for the lost gear. Soon we had four lines and a total of forty spreads fishing. King salmon wasted little time before they began striking. Their dark backs and rainbow scales glittered in the clear water as we pulled them in. From three in the morning to noon, we worked steadily hauling gear, bopping, gaffing, and cleaning fish. We took a few momentary breaks—me to vomit and Joe to shake his head for hiring such a wimp.

Despite the chaos, violence, and stress of my first king opener, I was completely smitten. It wasn't the money or the all-you-can-eat seafood buffet that kept me coming back each year; it was the people and the place. Through buckets of blood and slime, Joe and his wife Sandy became family. In 1971, when Joe was eighteen, he moved to the Elfin Cove, close to the northern limit of Chichagof Island. He built a cabin, bought a small skiff, and hand-trolled for salmon. At the end of his first season, he hadn't made enough money to cover gas and food. Sandy had hand-trolled all over Southeast and homesteaded on Kupreanof Island until one fateful night at a bar in Juneau. The two young fishermen ran into each other and got to talking. The next thing Sandy knew, Joe had invited himself to spend the winter with her, cut off from the rest of the world, on Kupreanof Island. The beer must have been particularly good and Joe devilishly charming because Sandy agreed.

The Craigs told me stories that left me in awe. A giant squid that surfaced when they were trolling with limbs so long you could drive a boat beneath a half coil of a tentacle. Twenty-foot rogue waves on an otherwise placid ocean. Their friend, the mysterious Raymond Lee, a now-deceased troller and recluse who sailed and shipwrecked all over the world. A humpback whale that got tangled in their anchor line and dragged their boat out into the big ocean. Sandy barely pausing from trolling to give birth to their son. The lost Tlingit village of Apolosovo in Surge Bay, where some believe that in July of 1741, Aleksei Chirikov, captain of the *St. Paul*, mysteriously lost fifteen crew members while trying to make contact with the settlement. The rumors of a long ago Tlingit summer camp on the Inian Islands that was wiped out by a hungry giant squid. Out here was a world unlike anything I'd encountered.

Joe Craig and me with a boatload of halibut aboard the
FV *Njord*. (Photo courtesy of Sandy Craig)

I began to build my own repertoire of experiences the more time
I spent trolling, longlining, and wandering the woods of Chichagof
and Yakobi Islands. A giant bull sea lion tearing apart a small
sea lion in a scuffle over a wounded salmon. A male killer whale
swimming benevolently with a large pod of Dall's porpoises. Brown
bear encounters that made my heart stop one moment only to fill
me with electricity the next. A humpback whale spy-hopping an
unsuspecting sea otter ten feet into the air. Befriending and fishing
with Debra Page and Bob-o Bell, who could win an award for being
a couple with a lifetime of unique, hardcore adventures. At the end
of each season, I caught a floatplane back to Juneau and would look
back at the Fairweather mountains and Cross Sound with a twinge
of nostalgia.

In 2012 I fished the big king opener with Debra on her boat the *Madame Ching*, named after an infamous female Chinese pirate. The winds were fierce, keeping trollers elsewhere in Southeast Alaska anchored up, but we were able to fish in the lee of the storms most days. It was some of the best fishing Joe, Sandy, Debra, and Bob-o had seen in their nearly forty seasons. By day eight, due to carpal tunnel from bopping and cleaning so many fish, I couldn't buckle my pants in the morning.

"Remedy for that is pissing on your hands," Bob-o joked when we tied up to his boat, the *Village Idiot*, in the afternoon.

A few days after the king opener was over, I was back on the *Njord* helping Joe and Sandy longline for their annual quota of halibut. Fishing had been good, and it looked to be a quick season. After bringing aboard the day's catch, Sandy and I baited hooks and stared at the verdant forest and mountain peaks as Joe drove home. In Elfin Cove, we gutted, gilled, and iced the halibut. Afterward, I borrowed their Zodiac and putted up Port Althorp. There was a place I wanted to visit before I returned to Juneau. I drove past sea otters, porpoises, humpback whales, and a huge, derelict Trident Cannery to a lonesome salt chuck. Easing into the protected inlet, the world became strangely tense and still. Raymond Lee used to anchor here to avoid the summer bustle in Elfin Cove. When dementia forced him into an assisted living home, he left his boat here amidst jumping salmon, prowling brown bears, and grazing deer. I motored to a granite boulder and tied the Zodiac off. Trudging amidst deer and grizzly tracks, I searched for the remains of his boat. In the two years since I last visited, the ocean and land had swallowed it.

Back in Elfin Cove, I drank beer, ate coho salmon, and laughed with Joe and Sandy. At three in the morning, we hopped onto the *Njord* and headed out onto Cross Sound to pull our two longline sets. Halibut after halibut flopped onto the boat until there was nowhere left to stand. The sound of Joe's bellowing laughter mixed with the gentle chugging of the diesel engine. Seagulls wafted on the wind hoping for a handout. The ocean was calm, and the Fairweather mountains beckoned savage and white.

"It's a bloody business," Sandy said as we slowly motored back to Elfin Cove, "but it's a good life."

A GOOD WEIGHT TO CARRY

"I'M GETTING TOO OLD FOR THIS," I said, resting against a steep, mossy slope, the straps of my pack cutting into my shoulders. My two brothers and I were carrying three blacktail bucks and camping gear off a mountain on Admiralty Island. They grunted in agreement. We'd had this conversation after successful alpine hunts since we were teenagers, though we'd developed different ways of training for hauling heavy loads. Luke and Reid climbed mountains, jogged, and cross-country skied. I, on the other hand, carefully monitored and charted my beer consumption to make sure I stayed twenty or thirty pounds overweight. The extra weight mimics a heavy pack and keeps me in peak shape for hunting season.

Over the years, I had tried all sorts of methods to haul meat. Early on, I was most concerned with looking cool. For my first buck, I took off my shirt and managed to sling the deer over my shoulders.

"This is how I pack deer!" I told my good pals Jesse Walker and Ed Shanley. I made it about ten yards before collapsing. The next few deer I made into deer-packs, something my dad had shown me how to do.

"I only do this if I have to," he had told me. "It's a lot easier to butcher the animal and use a backpack to carry the meat. You're also more likely to get shot by another hunter or have a bear jump on you if you're wearing a deer."

The easier, the smeezier. What would Hawkeye from *The Last of the Mohicans* do? He'd definitely take off his shirt, make the deer into a pack, and scoff at any hunter wearing a Kelty. I managed to pack out a small fork-horn in this manner but smelled like a deer for weeks afterward, something I was immensely proud of.

"You smell like a rutty, rotten deer," a high school classmate said in disgust.

"Thanks. It was a buck," I said. At that time of my life, the way I smelled was a pretty good indicator of what could be hunted or fished at the moment.

"Why do you keep taking off your shirt when we go hunting?" Luke asked the following hunting season, right after a spooked deer ran off. "It's weird, and you're so white you reflect light. I can't think of what else would have scared that deer."

Shamed, I put my t-shirt back on and embarked on a more practical approach to hunting and meat hauling. I learned that different hunts dictate a different approach to getting meat and keeping it in optimal condition, from the field into the freezer. Having a "meat plan" minimized the discomfort of hauling and, most importantly, contributed to every ounce of meat becoming a delicious meal when I returned home. Some folks swear by pack-boards, some external frame packs, while others use internal frame packs. For winter caribou hunts, some hunters bring a sled. For late season deer hunts at lower elevations, some hunters drag their deer to the beach. Every method has its pros and cons. For most of the meat hauling I do— deer and mountain goats in mountainous and brushy terrain and caribou on foot or skis—I rely on a big internal frame pack.

After the shot, I consider the temperature and duration of time before I can get meat cooled before I begin butchering. If it's warm and I'm more than a day away from getting meat cool, I keep the quarters intact and devote one game bag to neck meat and scraps. I always keep the liver and heart separate, in one game bag. After slogging back to base camp, I hang game bags from trees to keep meat aerated and out of the reach of critters. If I can hoist the meat high enough off the ground, I keep it at least one hundred yards away to minimize the chances of bears disrupting camp. On winter and mountain hunts, I often bury quarters or even entire carcasses in snow. It's a great way to keep meat in prime condition, although you risk the chance of attracting a variety of hungry animals. If hanging meat high in a tree is impossible and you're in bear territory, you're in a bit of a conundrum. Generally once I shoot an animal, I try to get out of the woods as quickly as possible. If it's legal and I'm not far from home, I like to bone out the quarters and ribs. It's amazing how much easier this makes for packing an animal.

In my early twenties, I befriended Mike, who would later become a respected mountain climbing guide, avalanche forecaster, and one of my favorite people to go hunting with. I had the privilege to go with Mike on his first successful Sitka blacktail hunt, and I have him to thank for one of my favorite meat-packing stories. We skiffed across to Admiralty Island in early August and, only having the day to hunt, hiked as fast as we could. Before running around in the mountains for a living, Mike played college soccer. Needless to say, my lungs and tendons were about to explode by the time we made it to the alpine. After sneaking around and peering over a number of ledges, we spotted a nice spike-fork bedded below. A few moments later, Mike bagged his first Sitka blacktail. What transpired afterward we still debate.

In August, as only bucks are legal for the taking, you are required by law keep to evidence of sex attached to a quarter. To do this, you have to keep a small patch of hide with the genitals attached to one quarter. I was hoping to get a deer that day too, so I offered quick skinning advice and ran off. I traversed the mountain until I noticed a herd of nearly a dozen deer on a steep slope above. I fell to the ground, trying to get a clean shot on a nice buck mixed up with a group of does. The deer grew tense and seemed about to bolt when a big buck appeared to the side. Resting the crosshairs behind his shoulder, I pulled the trigger, and deer ran in every direction. The big buck came sliding down the mountain so fast I had to dive out of its way. I thanked the animal then quickly quartered and loaded my pack with meat. Reunited with Mike, we began the arduous hike down to the beach.

Mountain guru Mike Janes and me in the alpine of northern Southeast Alaska. (Photo courtesy of Luke Dihle)

"I'm getting too old for this," I said during a rest. Mike looked like he was in pain, which was odd because he's about as tough as they come. Gradually he began to fall behind.

"You all right?" I asked.

"I'll hang in there," he muttered. We pushed through the guard timber to the beach in the late evening. The rugged mountains of the Coastal Range glowed across Stephens Passage. Two young brown bears splashed at the mouth of a stream. I lifted Mike's pack into the skiff and nearly threw out my back.

"Did you load your pack with rocks"? I asked. His deer had weighed at least thirty pounds less than the one I shot. "Your pack weighs more than mine."

"You said to keep the hide on the deer," Mike said, glowering, perhaps wondering if he'd just been hazed.

Eventually he forgave me, and now we laugh about it. I'm still not sure how he managed to fit the carcass of an adult buck in his pack, though.

Each August I look forward to hiking deer off mountains with my brothers, Dad, Mike, and other friends. Someday I may live to be too old to haul a deer to the beach from the mountains. Packing a caribou across miles of tussocks and hunting mountain goats with my brothers will be only something I can do in my memories. But something tells me the weight of the animals I've hunted will never really go away. Theirs is a good weight to carry.

FISHICTION

MANY FISHERMEN SUFFER from a compulsive, anxious, and even tortured relationship with fish. A recent article in *Today's Journal of Fishermen's Psychological Abnormalities*, entitled "Fishiction: Fact, not Fiction," says the relationship between fisherman and fish is far more complex and dangerous than originally thought. For millions of people, fish and fishing have become an addiction that frequently leads to balding, a variety of neuroses, and deviant behaviors. Scientists and clergy alike feel a big step has been made that there's finally a name for this affliction and are working on a cure.

I've struggled with many addictions—Big League Chew bubble gum, Cheddar Beddars, cream cheese, etc.—and can safely attest there's nothing worse than fishiction. A few months ago, for instance, even though I had a fair amount of salmon and halibut in my freezer, I drove through the darkness of night, howling wind, and pouring rain to my older brother Luke's garage. My brother had long wondered if someone was breaking into their house and taking their fish. I'd suggested the local meth-addicted PETA biker gang—the one I like to tell my nieces admonishing fairy tales about before they go to sleep—were stealing it for ritualistic purposes. I crept into his garage and was elbows deep in his freezer, cherry picking fillets of halibut and salmon, when his daughter Braith—the Brock Lesnar of six-year-olds—surprised me with a large stick she'd sharpened into a spear. Naturally, I was afraid. Who wouldn't fear a berserking child with no regard for life or limb, armed with a spear that in all likelihood had its tip smeared with the excretions of some extremely venomous endangered amphibian from the Amazon? I screamed, higher pitched than I'd like to admit, as she corralled me in the corner.

"Fishless fisherman, how dare you steal from my freezer!" she shrieked, running at me like a rabid cheetah about to tear down a gazelle. I flung frozen chunks of halibut at her until I was out of ammo then raised my arms in defeat. She had beaten me up several times in the past over much more minor offenses, so I knew this was not likely to end well.

"Ho, ho, ho! Don't you recognize me? It's Santa Claus!" I said, trying to think fast; it was dark after all, and Christmas was only a few months away. She'd told me a while back I looked like a young Santa. I could claim that global warming got my reindeer all confused and we'd mistaken Southeast Alaska for the North Pole, crashed, and were now in dire need of seafood to survive.

"Bjorn," Braith said and, much to my relief, set her spear aside. "Sit down. I think we should have a talk. What is it that makes you steal from our freezer?"

What ensued was a rather messy confession of my fishiction—I was near tears by the time I told her of how hard each day was, how I knew it was wrong and crazy, but I was losing sleep over fish and I couldn't stop raiding other people's freezers and standing for hours, fishing pole in hand, at the edge of the ocean waiting for the salmon to return. Braith was firm but understanding. When she demanded a fishing rod for her birthday, which was the following week, chills went down my spine. Would she turn out like me? A bohemian fisherman and petty fish thief?

That night as I paced my room, I prayed to Dagon, the fish god, to grant me serenity to accept the fish I'd lost, the courage to become a better fisherman, and the wisdom to stop coveting others' freezers. In the morning, I visited my friend Jesse Walker, a miner who has

Fish Doctor Jesse Walker and Brian Gilbertson, two soggy-bottom Southeast boys, with a couple spring king salmon. (Photo courtesy of Jesse Walker)

set up a small Past Fishing Regression Hypnotism business on the side. He claims it's an ancient form of therapy created to help those suffering from all sorts of fishing maladies. I was a little skeptical at first, since his office is actually his garage chock full of fishing rods, tackle, and pictures of fish, but after drinking a few beers, I felt remarkably at ease. The Fish Doctor, as Jesse likes to be called when he's in a professional capacity, had me sit next to some oily rags and rusty tools.

"Close your eyes. I'm going to count down from ten, and you're going to go back to when this neurosis began," the Fish Doctor said. When he got to five, his phone rang; I overheard the caller mentioning something about going trolling for winter kings. For a few moments afterward, there was rustling, clanging, and swearing. Then the sound of a door slamming and silence. I opened my eyes to see that Jesse had vanished. At first I was irritated and wondered if it had all been a ploy to fleece twenty bucks out of me. But as I stared at the walls plastered with photos of Jesse holding massive king salmon, their silver scales still alive with rainbows, I knew that this had all been planned, that leaving me alone in his garage while he pretended to go fishing was all part of my therapy. It must have been Jesse's way of telling me that my greatest demons had to be fought alone, that my fishiction was only in my mind, that it was something I had created in my misguided way of trying to make sense of the chaos of fish and fishing.

"You dirty dog!" I said, chuckling, but a pallor came over the room when I noticed his freezer just feet away. What was inside of it? Maybe there was smoked black cod or king? Maybe there were belly strips from sockeyes? Maybe halibut cheeks? A quick peek would do no harm. A few moments later, I stormed out of his house, my arms full of as many delicacies as I could carry. Jesse called me later that evening asking if I knew what happened to his winter stores. I blamed the local meth-addicted PETA biker gang, but I'm not sure he bought it.

I'm proud to say that it's been forty-two days since I last raided someone's freezer—which, if I'm honest, is mostly because my freezer is overloaded with other people's fish. Fishiction is something I and millions of other just have to live with. There's still no word of a cure, but I take comfort in knowing things will get easier when the salmon return this summer. Until then, you'll find me at the edge of the ocean, rod in hand, waiting.

MONARCH

IN THE WINTER OF 2012, Luke convinced me to put my name in the drawing for the Tok and Delta sheep hunts. There were just a few hours left before Fish and Game closed the registration. I'd never signed up for the draw, but I soon realized how much it was like gambling and why my brother and multitudes of other hunters are addicted to it. It's lucky Fish and Game limits the amount of hunts you can sign up for; otherwise, many folks would empty their bank accounts, become homeless, and panhandle solely for the chance to register for more.

When Fish and Game released the results a few months later, I saw I'd been picked for the late-season Delta hunt. I phoned Luke to tell him the good news.

"You no-good punk," he said. "I've been putting in for those sheep hunts for nearly fifteen years and have never been drawn."

Less than an hour later, Luke and our younger brother, Reid, called to proclaim they'd gotten time off from their wives and work to make the hunt. I hung up the phone feeling like I'd been thrown into a swift river and no longer had control of my life. If, for whatever reason, I decided not to make the hunt, I'd likely be excommunicated from my family, perhaps even burned at the stake.

All spring and summer my brothers trained for the hunt. Luke, convinced there was a correlation between eating healthy and having stamina, even bought a fancy juicer. I left town to commercial fish for a month, and when I returned, Reid had fallen victim to Luke's bad influence and had stopped drinking beer and taken up jogging. I was used to Luke being "healthy," but seeing my younger brother succumb to the fad was disturbing. Worried they might leave me behind in the woods, I took to carrying extra beer and fried foods on hikes as part of my training regimen. A few days before our departure, Reid and I started up a mountain at the same time as an incredibly fit ultra-runner. Reid recollects this man as being a pudgy, elderly chain smoker carrying an oxygen tank, but I have a better memory than he does. The three of us raced through the forest much like a sequence from the movie *The Last of the Mohicans*, except that I fell down a lot and we took frequent breaks, the ultra-runner to have a cigarette, me to wheeze, and Reid to have coughing fits that sounded oddly like "You're fat" and "You're slow."

"Man, you got a weird cold," I said between breaths. Reid, looking disgusted, shrugged. We pulled away from our competitor while he was adjusting the forty-pound oxygen tank he was wearing on his back.

"We whooped that skinny ultra-runner!" I said hours later when we reached the top of the three-mile hike. "I'm at the peak of my fitness level."

Toward the end of August, a couple days before the sheep hunt opened, my brothers and I took the ferry from Juneau to Haines. The second hunt in the Delta control area is open to motorized access. We hoped by hiking in the day before the opener, we'd be able to get a head start on less masochistic hunters who were using four-wheelers for a chunk of the approach. Rain splattered the windshield, and a wall of clouds hid the mountains. Not having music or scenery to look at, my brothers passed the time talking about sheep and making fun of me. I dreamed of the Delta Mountains. Though not as big or dramatic as other regions in the Alaska Range—Mount Kimball, at 10,300 feet, is the region's tallest peak—the Deltas are breathtaking. In my late teens and early twenties, I'd wandered much of the eastern Alaskan

Range, including the Delta Range. I remembered herds of sheep and rugged mountains, caribou and giant plateaus, the excitement of encountering grizzly bears and wolves, how surreal it was to nearly bump into a moose during a snowy night, insane displays of northern lights, and a host of other cherished—though not always pleasant in the moment—adventures. I felt I was on my way to go visit an old friend.

We drove into Tok late in the evening and met up with friends who'd just returned from a successful sheep hunt in the Wrangell Mountains. Studying the artistic lines and curves of the horns, I got excited. After many days of hiking and seeing several different non-legal sheep, these friends had spied a nice ram. They studied the sheep for an hour at just one hundred yards before deciding it was legal. Punishment for taking a ram that's not full curl is severe, something that made me a bit nervous. We unloaded a chest freezer at their house. If we lucked out and got a sheep early, we planned on processing and freezing it in Tok and then making another walk-in sheep hunt and then a walk-in caribou hunt in the two weeks before we'd return to Southeast. We left Tok in darkness and rain, driving north on the empty highway to a river we planned to follow into sheep country the next day.

The morning was crisp and clear as we walked through the taiga along a four-wheeler trail. Spruce grouse, collecting grit for their gizzards, flew up into the low branches of spindly black spruce trees. Mushrooms of all sorts, including prolific amounts of highly prized boletes, crowded the forest's edge. A large, heavy-bodied bird of prey winged quietly overhead. After a few miles, the trail petered out, and we followed the gravel bars of the river. We made multiple crossings, some almost waist deep. Rugged mountains rising out of the boreal forest quickened my pulse. Sheep country was almost within reach—well, actually, it was still about ten hours of hard hiking away, but that's what it felt like when I stared up at the expanse of wild peaks. In the afternoon, we clawed through miles of brush, slowly climbing a winding ridge that led away from the river and into the mountains.

"I'm not sure this is the ridge we want to be on," Reid said as we stared at an uninviting expanse of willows and bushes. We decided to descend a brushy slope, losing a thousand feet of hard-earned elevation, to get onto another ridge. Partway down, my brothers stopped in their tracks and whispered excitedly. A huge bull caribou on the other side of the canyon browsed the yellowing willows, slowly moving from one bush to the next like something that better belonged to the Pleistocene. Knowing Luke wanted a big bull, I encouraged him to shoot the mammoth. There were two more days left in the caribou season for the region.

"No way," Luke said. "That may be the biggest caribou I've ever seen, but a chance to hunt sheep here is a once-in-a-lifetime opportunity."

Other caribou appeared as we clambered down into a canyon. We rested a few minutes, Luke and Reid filtering water and me drinking straight out of the creek, before slowly climbing an un-consolidated and steep slope of mud and rocks. An hour later, we made the alpine, and I fell in an exhausted heap. Reid and Luke were annoyingly peppy—maybe there is a correlation between eating healthfully, exercising, and not being a fat pud. A pack of wolves howled from the bottom of the canyon, and caribou scattered from sight. In deep twilight, as Luke made a delicious dinner of hot dogs, noodles, and Indian spices, we watched two massive bull moose sky-lined on a ridge across the valley.

In the morning, we moved camp a few miles farther up onto a plateau near a small pool that would provide water for drinking and cooking. Mountains looking like perfect sheep habitat blotted out the horizon in the not-so-far distance. Beyond the six- and seven-thou-sand-foot peaks were jagged alpine monsters with glaciers clinging to near vertical faces and slopes. Hiking toward those shale-covered monoliths, I remembered why I loved the Delta Mountains so much. Two white specks stood out on a ridge. I paused and stared through my rifle's scope.

"Those look like sheep," I said. Luke got out his spotting scope and verified they were indeed sheep. We dropped out of sight, hik-ing along the steep edge of the plateau before down-climbing into a drainage that offered coverage. Caribou and fox tracks wended along the sandy bottom. An occasional small flock of ptarmigan, their feathers a mottled mixture of their summer and winter color phases, exploded into flight. We crawled to a small knoll, and Luke glassed the sheep again.

"There's two, four, six in all. They look pretty blocky. I'm guessing they're rams, but we're going to have get quite a bit closer before I can be sure," he said. We considered how to stalk the herd. Luke and Reid hunted sheep in the past and knew that the best way to stalk is coming down on them. Trying to get above the sheep with the amount of daylight we had left didn't seem like a viable option—it would take miles and hours of backtracking just to stay out of view before we'd have to traverse a series of mountains. Even spending the night out—not an attractive option with the amount of frost and ice on pools we'd seen that morning—didn't seem like it would work.

"Well, we can follow this drainage and see how close we can get. If they're rams and any look full curl, we'll go from there," I suggested. We worked our way up the winding drainage for a few miles before creeping to a vantage point.

"They're rams!" Luke whispered excitedly as he peered through his spotting scope. "One, maybe two, look like they could be full curl!"

The shrub willows vanished into gray shale and low-growing grasses as we inched closer. The wind was good, with a gentle breeze flowing down the valley. At seven hundred yards, we paused and studied the small herd as they slowly grazed grass in a large shale-covered bowl. Watching through the spotting scope, I was struck by how regal and otherworldly the rams looked. Now I understood why my dad, Luke, Reid, and so many others suffer so acutely from sheep fever. Here we were, in one of the wildest and most beautiful places on earth, slowly closing in on six magnificent animals. Just being near them was a gift and the makings of a good memory. I considered refusing to shoot, both to see how my brothers would react and to get back at them for making me the butt of their jokes. I'm not going to lie, though—studying the boss ram, I felt the electricity of the hunt building. Slowly, we whittled away at the distance, hiding behind boulders and careful to move slowly and only when the rams were out of view. When the opportunity arrived, we ran up a steep slope and then clambered forward until the first ram came into view.

"Two hundred and fifty yards," Luke said after he checked his range finder. I tried to calm my thundering heart. It was within range. On advice from my dad, who had made three sheep hunts in the Wrangell Mountains in the 1980s, I practiced shooting my 7mm Magnum at three hundred yards before the hunt.

"You might only get one chance at a full-curl ram, and it's likely to be a long shot," Dad had said before recounting, in almost a religious tone, a couple of his favorite adventures he'd had with his sheep-hunting pal, Greg Turner.

I studied the ram carefully for five minutes, trying to gauge whether or not it was full curl. It looked close, but I was looking up at the ram. From this vantage point, a sheep's horns always look like they have more of a curl than they actually do.

"I think it's seven-eighths," I whispered back to my brothers, both of whom appeared to be shaking with excitement. Suddenly, the rest of the herd stepped into view.

"There's the boss!" Luke hissed. "He looks full!"

He sure looked more than full curl, but what if that was because I was looking up at him? Or what if my eye boogers made his horns look legal? Or what if I was hallucinating because I did psychedelics once when I was a teenager? As I agonized whether or not to shoot, the sheep slowly worked their way up the mountain, grazing as they went. Luke listed the distance. Two hundred seventy yards. Two hundred eighty yards. Two hundred ninety yards. Three hundred yards.

"Would you shoot him?" I asked Luke.

"Yes, but you have to make your own decision," he whispered back. Slowly, I slid my fleece onto a rock, eased my rifle atop, and counted breaths. Judging the rest as solid, I chambered a round and waited for the boss ram to turn broadside. I aimed about ten inches above where I thought his heart was and, gently exhaling, squeezed the trigger. At the crack of the shot, he staggered. It's a testament to his strength that he was able run sixty yards uphill after being lunged before he wobbled and keeled over. A few of the other rams stayed close, seemingly reluctant to leave.

Luke let out a barbaric howl that echoed off the mountains as I knelt with the ram's heavy head in my hands. Traveling so far to kill such a beautiful creature inspired strange and humbling emotions. Between commercial fishing, past stints trapping, and lots of meat

My brothers and me with a ram taken in the eastern Alaska Range.

hunting, I'd become pretty cold when it came to killing. Staring at the magnificent ram, I acutely felt the sadness of the hunt, something I hadn't experienced in years. Mostly, though, I just felt grateful to be in the Delta Mountains with my two best friends in the presence of such an awesome animal. Silently, I thanked the ram before we set to butchering.

On the hike back to camp, we were treated with the company of dozens of caribou, several of which were nice bulls. They ran and swirled around us, the bulls tilting their antlers backwards and gallantly trotting with clacking tendons. Luke and Reid were tempted. Thankfully, the thought of the additional weight of packing a bull twenty-five miles out to the road quelled their urge to pull the trigger. We made it to camp in the late evening. Tired and happy, we sat down to a dinner of heart and pasta.

In the morning, after we boned the ram out, we traveled by compass and GPS through a thick bank of fog. Caribou, looking ghost-like in the gray, ran circles around us. Emerging from the clouds, we took a different route down to tree line. A young bull caribou tempted Reid about three or four miles from the river bottom. It seemed disturbingly unaware of the threat we presented.

"We got two more hunts," Reid said, sighing. If he filled his tag now, he wouldn't be able to make the Fortymile hunt we were planning. "This would be more like murdering than hunting anyway."

The boreal forest smelled of fermenting cranberries as we hiked along the edge of impressive series of beaver dams. We stumbled into a big bull moose thirty yards away. Instead of running, the massive animal just stared as we watched him all googly eyed. In the late evening, we set up camp on the river's gravel bar and built up a large fire. Luke and Reid placed rocks in the coals before setting a side of ribs wrapped in tin foil atop. Twilight came over the taiga as the meat hissed and splattered. The sheep, even without seasoning, was delicious. After finishing each rib, we tossed the bones into the swirling current of the river.

"We may be the luckiest folks alive," Luke said as stars dotted the night's canopy and the fire burned low. Both Reid and I agreed.

Dear Patagonia,

Please Hire Me as a Fashion Designer

It was once believed that people who went out of their way to travel into the wilderness did so to ponder the depths of their souls, test their mettle, and write flowery poetry. This is not true. You, I, and everyone else know the real reason is to be seen in and justify buying snazzy clothes. These days the trails of national parks are hotter than the fashion runways of New York and Paris.

For years I dreamed of becoming a gear model. These aspirations were crushed when a photographer working for REI told me my complexion and body type just weren't right for the fast-paced and cutthroat outdoor fashion industry. I accept I may not be cut out to be a gear model, but I believe I have what it takes to become an outdoor fashion designer. If you choose to hire me, Patagonia, I will greatly aid your company with my innovative and bold vision. What follows is a brief sample of some of my product ideas.

1. ARCTIC PARKAS: Through the years, the arctic parka has been greatly shortened in length. When I bought my first parka from a thrift shop in Fairbanks, it went down to my knees. Friends claimed it was actually a dress, but I think they were just jealous. These days parkas rarely go below the beltline—getting frostbite on your nether regions has never been so hip. Why not take it a step further and make

parkas that end above the belly button—it was cool in the 1980s, and I'd be willing to bet with the right models we could reestablish the trend. Also, how about arctic t-shirts, tank tops, and sports bras? We could market the down feathers from endangered birds like the pelagic emu to promote the preservation of the species.

2. GROOMING PRODUCTS: I notice few gels, lotions, or other grooming products in your catalog. It's time for the myth of wilderness wanderers being no-frills Neanderthals to end. There's a seldom-known rumor that John Muir, father of the wilderness movement, was a diva who used a variety of gels to keep his devilishly good-looking locks and bearish beard long, glossy, and flowing. I've come up with a number of products that may interest you. My personal favorite is an organic salve with a bear bile base (bought from hunters who promote the sustainable poaching and harvesting of bear gallbladders) that does wonders for blackheads.

I model a cool hat. (Photo courtesy of MC Martin)

3. ORGANIC AND RECYCLED THONGS: One of the biggest complaints I hear from adventurers is how, after about a week in the wilds, they no longer feel attractive. I suggest Patagonia brings sexy back to the wilderness with a line of moisture-wicking, organic, and completely recycled thongs. There's no shortage of brothels where we could attain truckloads for next to nothing.

4. WILD SCENTS: Consider a line of perfumes and colognes based off animals' scent glands. So far I've bottled "Mustelid Desire," a real slump buster for those having trouble getting dates. "Ursine Obsession" is a great way to attract a partner from miles away—just remember to urinate frequently in public areas. "Hot Carnal Canis" works wonders in bringing back the heat to a boring marriage. After the salmon return to lay their eggs, I'll also have the Ray Troll–inspired "Spawn or Die," a must-have for any true romantic. It'll likely be the biggest thing since Internet dating.

5. TANNING SPRAYS AND RASH CREAMS: One of the coolest things about going on an expedition is getting a hand and face tan, ingrown hairs, chafed thighs, and a wide variety of other rashes. What if we created a tanning spray specifically for hands and face? A cream that caused rashes without even having to go outside would surely be a big hit in the outdoor industry.

I have dozens of other great ideas and am happy to send you my entire portfolio if you're interested in taking part in the cutting edge of outdoor fashion. Don't miss this opportunity.

Sincerely,
Bjorn Dihle

ADAK CARIBOU

THE WORD *caribou* sends shivers down my spine and makes me want to drop what I'm doing and migrate somewhere cold and wild. It also makes me hungry. So when my family told me we were going to Adak to look for grass-fed caribou, I was excited.

"The biggest bulls in the world used to come from Adak," Luke, my older brother, said as we took our seats on an Alaska Airlines plane. "But it's a meat hunt now. For one reason or another, the big bulls—or at least their antlers—seem to have vanished."

The lure of Adak, its 275 square miles shaped by solitude, violence, and change, extended well beyond hunting opportunities. Its history alone was spellbinding. For thousands of years, Aleut people lived on the island, paddling kayaks and umiaks up, down, and beyond the thousand miles of the Aleutian chain. Vitus Bering's tragic but amazing voyage in 1741 to Alaska led to a tsunami of Russian fur traders and devastating effects on the Aleuts. In June of 1942, the Japanese Imperial Army invaded neighboring islands Attu and Kiska, resulting in the first time enemy forces occupied American soil since the War of 1812. Aleut people were relocated to Southeast Alaska for the remainder of the war. A brutal, often forgotten fifteen-month battle known as "The Thousand-Mile War" ensued. Adak rapidly became the site of a US military airstrip and base as well as being the main staging point to take back Attu and Kiska. During the Cold War, it acted as a military outpost, sometimes manned by as many as six thousand folks. In 1997 the military pulled out, shrinking the population to around three hundred and turning Adak into a ghost town of mythical proportions. Big bulls or not, I felt lucky to get a chance to wander the island's deserted streets, stormy mountains, and valleys. A caribou or two would be a bonus.

"The population has gotten so out of control it might implode," Luke said.

"There's got to be some monster bulls left in the herd," said Reid, our younger brother.

"You guys can go chase caribou. I'm going fishing," Dad said dreamily.

"I hear there are also fantastic black-sand beach walks and amazing bird-watching opportunities!" I piped in.

"You go walk on beaches and go birding. We're going hunting," Reid said.

"What if we birdwatch half the time and hunt the other half?" I asked. My brothers reclined their seats and shoved their baseball caps down over their eyes.

There are no large terrestrial mammals native to Adak, so to give military personnel hunting opportunities, eighty-six newborn caribou calves from the Nelchina caribou herd were captured in the foothills of the Talkeetna Mountains and shipped to the island in the late 1950s. When the calves were weaned and ready to fend for themselves, the twenty-three survivors were released. With no predators, mild winters, few bugs, and plenty of browse, the population took off. A 2012 aerial survey counted between 2,500 and 2,800 caribou. Too many, according to biologists who are concerned the caribou may be adversely affecting the unique ecosystem of the island. Some call the caribou of Adak an invasive species, and there have been rumors of certain agencies wanting to eradicate the herd.

Five hours later, the plane shuddered in a storm as I stared at a verdant volcano. A red can buoy rolled amidst the waves of the white-capped Bering Sea. The plane slammed onto the runway and pulled up next to a sign that read, "Welcome to Adak, the Birth Place of the Winds." Long-faced hunters waiting to fly home milled in the waiting room, speaking quietly about how few caribou they'd seen and how heinous the weather had been. Cynthia and Joe, the owners of Little Michael Lodges, greeted us warmly. After getting us a truck and showing us to the condo where we were staying, they left us to collect our thoughts and watch the rain fall as the wind shook abandoned buildings. Not knowing what to do in a fancy condo, I gorged on Cheez-Its and whiskey.

The following morning, while I was in the bathroom feeling like a natural disaster, an earthquake registering seven on the Richter scale struck less than one hundred miles to the south. I'm pretty sure my family thought the shaking walls had something to do with my aftershocks from the night before. Cynthia stopped by to check on us as we loaded our packs in the truck. Staying in a condo and being checked on felt strangely comforting yet frighteningly civilized. I grabbed a couple handfuls of Cheez-Its for breakfast as we drove into the gray dawn, past abandoned homes and barracks to the end of the road. Fog swirled over green mountains, and waterfalls poured down cliffs. Eagles, bored with tearing at humpy salmon carcasses lining creeks, eyed us hungrily. My brothers climbed a steep hill and began jogging along a bluff above a lake.

"They're maniacs," Dad muttered as we struggled to keep up.

"Hold up!" I said, wheezing. They froze, thinking I'd spotted caribou up in the mountains. A small brown-and-white bird was perched on a nearby rock. I tore out my bird book and began flipping pages. "Nope. Nope. Nope. Bullseye! Guys, it's a Lapland longspur!" I said. I looked up to see my brothers halfway up a mountain pass, disappearing into the fog.

Pelting rain and fifty-mile-per-hour winds buffeted us as we felt our way down a wet, grassy slope to a valley covered in fog. Dad knelt to pick up a handful of rusty cartridges from a small tussock. It was hard to read the make, but we were pretty sure they were .30 caliber. In the afternoon the fog lifted, revealing a lake surrounded by grassy mountains.

"Caribou!" Reid hissed, gesturing at a cow, calf, and yearling a half mile away. Adak caribou are significantly larger and mature more quickly than caribou elsewhere in the state. Female yearlings generally get pregnant, and there's been at least one documented case of a calf conceiving. Luke and Reid jumped into a stream then crawled to the top of a knoll. Dad and I followed behind, examining the flora and speculating on whether or not the lake and creek had trout. Reid gestured wildly at tiny specks in a mountain draw. After making a plan for a stalk, we kept low until we were out of view. I was excited enough to jog, an activity I find utterly undignified. Caribou tracks, trails, and pellets laced the hillside. A few hundred yards above me, Reid crawled up to the edge of the herd. While he was getting a rest on a nice meat bull, a cow emerged less than thirty yards away. Remembering what Fish and Game said about wanting hunters to take cows, he quickly shot. The herd, as sure-footed and graceful as Dall sheep, scattered across the steep mountain face. Reid happily rested his hand on the big cow's belly. Snow buntings and Lapland longspurs avoided swooping peregrine falcons as we packed meat back to the truck.

Each day we wandered for miles, generally in storms, searching for caribou. At night we feasted and drank. I shot a 170-pound yearling high in the mountains in a gale. Luke shot a young bull deep in a valley that seemed to belong to a lost world. We didn't have to worry about bears while we processed meat, a sharp departure from our experiences in Southeast Alaska. Taking a break from hunting, Dad caught cohos and rainbow trout, adding a little variety to our nightly dinners of heart and backstrap.

Early one day, beneath a blue sky, we stashed sleeping gear next to a giant barrel emergency shelter. Reid and I took advantage of the weather and made good time to the slopes above Teardrop Lake. Rugged black mountains rose above the pale blue expanse of the Bering Sea. The vista was so dramatic, we forgot we were hunting and just stared. A herd of thirty, along with one larger bull, moved across a mountain and roused us from our stupor. We descended a ravine and crawled to the top of a knoll but were blocked from the main herd by six cows. We crawled within a hundred yards of the six and debated whether or not to shoot. I knew Fish and Game was right to want hunters to shoot cows, but I've always had an aversion to taking female animals.

Dad looks out on the landscape of Adak Island.

"Let's try to cut off that bull," Reid said. After climbing above a valley we hoped the herd might be following, we waited a good thirty minutes before giving up on the caribou showing. Later, we caught up with Luke and Dad on a mountainside.

"We chased a cow with a broken leg but couldn't get a shot," Dad said. While chatting, Reid and I jumped simultaneously. Two miles away in a marsh near the lake, a bull, the biggest we'd seen on Adak, stood by itself. I'm a meat hunter, but I was tired of listening to Luke and Reid constantly banter over who'd taken bigger bucks and bulls. This brotherly competition began as a joke, but over the years it had evolved into something similar to a professional wrestling match. It got worse the previous year when Reid married into the Yalipu clan of the Micmac First Nation in Newfoundland. *Yalipu*, meaning "snow-shoveler," is the origin for the word *caribou*. He really thought he was hot stuff after that. Even Luke and Reid's wives frequently dropped low blows about the other husband's hunting abilities. I'm never invited to participate in the horseplay, which makes me insecure and bitter. So, as Reid and I ran along ridges, alpine slopes, and down ravines, I schemed of ways to increase my odds of getting a shot on the bull. Three caribou swirled in circles in front of us, at times coming within thirty yards. We waited, hoping they wouldn't spook the bull. When they moved off, we rushed to the hill we thought the bull was on the other side of. After a rapid crawl, the caribou appeared majestic and tense against the rustling grass and the lake's shimmering blue waters.

"Take him!" Reid, a better man than me, hissed. I chambered a round and, as the bull turned to the side, took a deep breath and gently squeezed. Though his rack wasn't huge, his body was by far the largest we'd seen during our wanders in Alaska and Canada. Kneeling next to him, I gave thanks. Reid and I quickly began butchering.

In the late evening, as clouds settled atop the mountains, I set about making a dinner of heart and pasta. Dad was just about to unscrew the whiskey bottle when a small herd of caribou appeared, moving across the hillside.

"Guess this is going to have to wait," he said, throwing a few things in his pack before chasing after Luke and Reid. In the twilight, they crawled behind boulders. Slowly, the herd moved their way. When the animals paused, realizing something was up, Dad made a nice quartering shot on a young bull. Bloody and bushed, they found their way back to camp in darkness. We celebrated with heart and whiskey.

"This is Valhalla," Luke said. "I could do this forever."

The rest of our time in Adak passed like a dream. We walked beaches, watching harbor seals, sea otters, and eider ducks rolling in the Bering Sea. Storm petrels rose on the wind then dove into the water. Black oyster catchers, harlequin ducks, and sand pipers stood on lava rocks as the ocean rose and fell at their feet. Rock ptarmigan croaked from the grass, inciting Luke and Reid to give chase with a .22 pistol. We wandered dirt streets through abandoned, creaking neighborhoods. On many buildings, the siding was torn away and windows were broken by storms.

"Adak just doesn't add up," Reid said as the sun set beyond a neighborhood of deserted white trailers. "It'd be a perfect place for a zombie movie."

Early the next morning we hiked back to Teardrop Lake. The

weather was unusually fair as we lay glassing a cow walking through the lake's shallows. With each step she took, the water exploded. After walking to the lake's shore, we realized why. The water was teeming with spawning sockeye salmon. I watched the red salmon while Luke and Reid, eager to bring more meat home, planned a stalk on a small group of caribou bedded down on the hillside above. They followed a ravine and crawled through the grass to the edge of a knoll, ending the hunt by taking a cow and a young bull.

On the last day, Reid and Luke went looking for ptarmigan. Dad and I recuperated by reading and walking the beach looking for puffins. Mountains rose from the ocean into clouds, making me wish I had more time to explore this strange and beautiful place. In the late afternoon, we picked Luke and Reid up in the rain and wind. They were ecstatic over their day of wandering.

"We saw the white wizard!" They shook their heads as if they still couldn't believe it. "There's definitely at least one humongous bull left on Adak. He let us get in easy shooting range off a four-wheeler trail! Man, I'm glad I didn't have my rifle."

We loaded our meat into totes and hauled them to the airport. A new crop of wide-eyed hunters disembarked the plane wondering what they'd gotten into. The nearly empty cabin rattled in the wind and pouring rain as we taxied onto the runway. Luke and Reid planned their next hunt then began arguing over who'd gotten a bigger buck the previous year. As we rose into the clouds, I thanked the island and its caribou.

THE CONSTANT FISHERMAN SYNDROME

THALEN JANES, a two-and-a-half-year-old fisherman, stood on a rock, fishing pole in hand, screaming as a three-inch Dolly Varden swung in the air. Irritated that I'd been fishing longer and only caught sea slugs, I feigned a congratulations. He whooped, hollered, and nearly fell into the ocean as his dad released the fish.

"Did you see the size of that fish?" Thalen asked my girlfriend, MC, gesturing with his hands spread as far apart as he could manage.

"A real whopper! Hey Bjorn, why can't you catch me a fish?" she asked.

"Cast over there," Thalen said to me, pointing to where a Dolly just surfaced. I cast in the opposite direction, snagged a rock, and spent the next few minutes lecturing the young fisherman on the proper technique of freeing a lure from the bottom. Thankfully, he was too engrossed with sticking his finger in a green sea anemone to see me break my line.

"I'm worried about Thalen," I said to MC as we drove to our friends Jesse and Monika Walker's house. "He's not even three years old and he's already got a bad case of the Constant Fisherman Syndrome."

Thalen, along with many folks in Southeast Alaska, suffered from this mania. The more obvious symptoms include the need to talk about fishing at home, work, or even while out fishing; a compulsion for lying and beer drinking; cravings for strange odors, including old bait and outboard fumes; fits of anger and irrational behavior when outfished by another angler; the need to drag a herring or spoon through the water, be it a mud puddle or ocean; an infatuation with fish of all types, often outrivaling interest in the opposite sex, eating, sleeping, etc.; reliance upon other people who are similarly affected; ambivalence and even abhorrence toward people who are not affected. Psychologists are only beginning to document and grasp the deeper connotations of why so many men, women, and children cannot put the fishing pole down. Their burgeoning research will likely revolutionize our understanding of Alaskan psychology in the next few years.

I feared Thalen's seemingly innocent fixation could turn into a really nasty case of the Constant Fisherman Syndrome. His dad, Mike, my longtime pal, had even taken the hooks off lures so Thalen and his big brother, Corder, could cast in the house. A seemingly benign activity, but eventually those boys were going to tire of catching each other and their little sister. They might start acting out, or worse, become depressed. You can't feed a tiger vegetables and expect it to survive. Thalen's obsession with fishing was all fine and good at the moment, but what'll happen when he's expected to fit into society, hold down a job, and raise a family? I planned to phone Mike and talk about staging an intervention.

"You're just making this up because you're jealous he outfished you," MC said after I'd related my concerns.

"Not true! Constant Fisherman Syndrome affects nearly one out of the two people in the state. Even my nieces are exhibiting symptoms. Adella can fillet a salmon better than I can, and she's in kindergarten. The other day Kiah told me she caught a king salmon, and you know what? It was actually a humpy. Fishing is teaching her to lie."

"There's nothing wrong with liking to fish or exaggerating a bit. Remember how you convinced me to date you?"

"But that fish really was that big!"

Thalen Janes biding his time until salmon season begins.
(Photo courtesy of Mike Janes)

"Sure it was. Too bad you didn't have a camera and no one else saw it."

"You know I don't take trophy pictures, and I always let the big ones go. That's beside the point anyhow. Thalen could easily turn out like Jesse and Thrash," I said, referencing two good friends who suffer from the syndrome worse than anyone I knew. For many years, during spring and summer, Jesse would wake every day of the workweek at four then troll until seven and be to work at seven thirty. After work he would troll until dark. On weekends he'd troll from four in the morning until dusk. If you called his phone during salmon season, you'd likely get his voicemail: "Hi, this is Jesse. Sorry for not answering. I'm out slaying king salmon and keeping the world safe for democracy. Leave a message, and I'll get back to you."

And Thrash, well, I've never met a man more preoccupied with hunting and fishing. Sometimes it seemed like he could get inside the minds of fish and convince them to bite his lure. If someone mentioned PETA, he wouldn't make a derogatory crack or an angry remark. He'd just shake his head and sadly whisper, "Man, why would anyone want to take away fishing and hunting? They must not have had anyone take them when they were young. Those poor fools, they just don't know any better."

I have other friends suffering from the Constant Fisherman Syndrome. There's "I Just Fish" Jon, originally from Vermont, who stood up in the middle of a college biology lecture and yelled, "I can't take it anymore! I'm moving to Alaska!" He dropped out of school, flew across the continent, and found reprieve in the company of the likes of Jesse and Thrash. There's Brian, an expert woodsman, who doesn't smile, feel, or say anything unless he's out hunting or fishing or in the woods. There's Ed, an Irish philosopher, subject to fly-fishing so hard it gives him the occasional flare-up of tendonitis. There's Ben, who hand-trolls in spring and summer, occasionally taking time off to go explore streams in search of steelhead and to write poems about fish. Occasionally they all get together and go fishing. It's the Southeast Alaska equivalent of Burning Man, but a lot wilder and more productive.

"There nothing wrong with Jesse or Thrash," MC said as we pulled into the driveway.

"You're probably right. They've both become more moderate in recent years," I said. When we walked into the Walker's residence, Jesse was sitting on the couch clutching a fishing rod, watching a fishing television show, and talking on the phone to someone about fishing. Thrash was there too, covered in fish slime, holding the fillet of a king salmon in one hand and yelling about a bigger fish that got away.

"Any luck?" they asked me.

"One real big one, but I let it go. Got more fish in the freezer than I can eat at this point," I said. MC gave me a dirty look but was good enough not to say anything. Later that night, I got tired of looking at fish pictures on the Internet and grabbed a fishing pole. I walked down to the duck pond to cast for a bit, hoping that it might make me feel better about being outfished earlier.

"Poor Thalen, this is your future," I said. For a moment, right when my rod bent wildly and a hysterical duck erupted into the night, I felt no pain.

DEERSLAYER

"GET ANY DEER?" MC asked as I brushed snow off myself and stumbled through the doorway. It was late December, deer season was almost over, and our freezer could use a bit more meat.

"Nope, but Reid got another nice buck," I said, dropping my snow-encrusted, blood-soaked pack atop her pile of shoes and boots.

"How come your little brother gets so many more deer than you?"

"I fell today," I said, showing her a half-inch scratch on my forearm. "It was really far. My whole life flashed before my eyes, and all I saw was you."

"Ohhh, sit on the couch! I'll bring you a beer."

I lay moaning like a sea lion for some time until the phone rang. It was my dad seeing if I felt like taking my rifle for a walk in a few days. I said yes. There are few things I'd rather do than crawl through brush, gloom, thirty-mile-per-hour winds, snow, and rain searching for deer.

"Why do we do this?" he said as we drove through darkness, the truck shuddering in a blizzard, toward one of our rifle-walking spots on Douglas Island.

"What else would we do?" I wondered.

After hiking by headlamp, we split up and entered the creaking, swaying, dripping rainforest. First light revealed the tracks of a doe and fawn traveling through thick brush. A short while later, fresh wolf tracks wended through snowy blueberry bushes and around windfalls, paralleling the base of the mountain. I slowly plodded through snow, climbing a series of benches until I reached a plateau where the flash of a bolting buck's antlers two weeks prior still made me a bit tingly. The sign there was old, so I slowly worked my way down, doing my best to keep the swirling wind from carrying my scent—a cross between cheese and wet dog—where I was hunting. Late in the short day, a deer appeared like a ghost beneath giant spruce and hemlock trees. I slowly raised my rifle and studied the animal. It had no antlers and looked small, maybe a yearling. After it traversed the hillside, I approached and examined its little tracks. It stared back warily with its ears cocked wide. With less than an hour of light left in the day, I bid the deer a good winter, sat on a snowy log, and watched the forest shuddering in the dark gray. When a chill crept in, I hightailed it to Dad's and my rendezvous point.

"Anything?" I asked when I came upon him standing next to a rushing creek.

"One fawn. No matter how hard I tried, I couldn't make it grow antlers," he said, as we hiked through the darkness back to the truck.

At home, MC asked if I had any luck. I shrugged, and she mumbled something about our imaginary child not having enough to eat to make it through the winter.

Getting skunked doesn't get me down. I have a long history of not getting deer and other game. In fact, I'm close to having an Alaskan grand slam for critters I've not shot and scared off. I also have a long history of inadvertently preventing other people from getting game. It was only recently that Luke forgave me for saving so many animals moments before he was going to shoot them. PETA needs to forget all their naked celebrity photo campaigns and simply hire a bunch of hunters like me to wander around the woods scaring off game from hunters like Luke. We'd be cheaper, easier to work with, and more effective. And it would be good for the celebrities too, as they wouldn't have to starve themselves and spend so much time and money cultivating their looks.

While I've blown stalks on critters numerous times for Luke, there is one occasion that I'd like to illustrate to PETA just in case they like my idea and want to pay me to go hunting. My family calls it the "sausage incident," and though two decades have passed since it happened, Luke and Dad still talk about it frequently.

The story begins well enough. Dad took Luke and me into the mountains of Douglas Island on an August deer hunt. Wanting to teach his sons to be tough, he brought very little food. A wise fatherly decision for sure, but it backfired a few days later when he and Luke spotted a buck bedded down with two does at the edge of a bowl. As I was a clumsy asthmatic porker with thick, perpetually fogged glasses, Luke and Dad left me with their packs to make a stalk. Seconds quickly turned to eons as my stomach grumbled and twisted in hunger. The last of our food was a summer sausage that Luke and I had spent hours fantasizing about. They wouldn't notice a small bite, I convinced myself as I pulled it from Dad's pack. One bite turned into two, then three. Soon I felt disgustingly full, but wanting to prove I had willpower, I polished the sausage off. Maybe they'd forget we'd ever brought it in the first place. This was unlikely. I needed to do something fast to make up for it. Through the blur and fog of my glasses, I became convinced a deer had emerged from the jack pines on the far side of the bowl. Without another thought, I grabbed my bow and, despite feeling too full to exert myself, stumbled in the direction of my quarry.

Meanwhile, a few hundred yards below, Luke and Dad were setting up for a shot on a nice fork-horn. Suddenly, the deer looked up the hill, stood, and bolted into the forest. I shrugged and waved at my dad and brother, who looked quite angry for some reason. I'm still not sure what spooked those deer. While moving from bush to bush, I was careful about wind direction and staying low. Electricity wisped through the air. I nocked an arrow. Slowly, I rose to my knees and squinted at the deer through the fog of my glasses. The tenseness of the moment was nearly unbearable. This was the moment of truth. This was when I went from a boy to becoming a man. My family would forget the sausage and hoist me onto their shoulders. When I walked off the mountain tomorrow, my dad and brother carrying the big buck I'd killed, everything would be different. Perhaps they'd hold a banquet and give me the nickname of Deerslayer. Shaking, I exhaled and slowly pulled the bow back.

There is a mysterious yet common phenomenon in hunting when an animal suddenly turns into a stump or rock. Many physicists have completed studies on these events, and still no good explanations exist on what causes them. Some theorists suggest time portals, wormholes to other universes, or global warming. I have my own idea involving complicated mathematical formulas proving that certain animals, most often ones I'm hunting, have the molecular ability to transform into stumps and rocks, but it needs more work before I publish it.

Somehow the deer I'd been stalking turned into a stump. Proud of myself nonetheless, I returned to my starved-looking dad and brother and regaled them with stories. For some reason, they didn't share my enthusiasm.

A Sitka blacktail doe in the mountains of Admiralty Island.

A FEW HOURS OF PAIN
FOR A WINTER
OF GOOD EATING

I'VE BEEN OBSESSED with caribou and the tundra, mountains, and forests they inhabit for as long as I can remember. The origin of the word *caribou* comes from the name of Newfoundland's Micmac First Nation clan, the Yalipu. It translates as "snow-shoveler"— caribou shovel through the snow with their sharp hooves to access lichens and other vegetation. Naturally, I took it as a good omen when my little brother, Reid, married a Newfoundlander who happens to be a member of the Yalipu clan. I suggested they honeymoon in the Arctic, perhaps follow a herd migrating from its winter grounds in the interior of Alaska to its calving grounds on the coastal plain. For some reason, they elected to go to Hawaii.

Lucky for me, I was born in Alaska, into a family that doesn't know how to talk about much other than hunting, fishing, and wildlife. In the spring of 2014, my older brother, Luke, came up with a grand plan of making back-to-back walk-in Dall sheep hunts and, if we had time, a caribou hunt as well. Months before, while drinking beers and staring at maps, it seemed almost too easy. By the third beer, it didn't even seem sporting. I suggested a handicap of some sort—maybe attaching fifteen-pound weights to our ankles. Luke and Reid took a more irrational approach, consisting of exercising and eating healthfully. When they encouraged me to do the same, I laughed.

"Look at the toughest guys: Russell Crowe, Denzel Washington, and Liam Neeson. Do any of those guys train? I doubt it. They just go into a room and beat up a dozen or so armed jerks half their age. Neeson once trekked across the frozen Arctic in blue jeans, fistfighting demon wolves the entire way, with zero training," I argued.

In early September, we'd made two sheep odysseys covering more than 120 miles of some of the most beautiful mountain country in the world. At the end of the second hunt, we still had a few days before we had to return home. We left our sheep meat in a friend's freezer in Tok and drove north into Fortymile country; caribou season opened the next day. Willows and aspens blazed yellow and red. Valleys were filled with the smell of fermenting cranberries. Snow crept down ancient shale-covered mountains. Reid and Luke shouldered their packs and followed a faint four-wheeler trail into desolate rolling hills. There was none of the excitement I generally felt at the beginning of a hunt. I limped behind, fighting the desire to lie down in the mud and take a nap.

"You sure you guys want to do this?" I asked when I caught up. In reply, they grumbled like constipated brown bears just woken from hibernation.

I moped along, considering adding a little something extra special to Luke's dinner tonight—maybe some caribou pellets or bear poop. Three walk-in hunts with no rest in between had been his idea, after all. Maybe I could find some centipedes. Luke gestured toward a hill. "Years ago, I met an old timer resting there. He had his head down, with a load of meat on his back. He looked utterly spent. I asked if he was all right, and he just smiled. Kind of had a twinkle in his eye. Said something about how a few hours of pain for a winter of good eating was a good deal."

I pushed away my evil scheming and instead recited the mantra, "A few hours of pain for a winter of good eating," as we hiked through a forest burnt to charcoal from one of the area's many forest fires. We crossed a tussock field, gained access to an alpine ridge, and climbed a scree-covered mountain. At the summit, the bleached-white antler shed of a large bull lay like a religious icon beneath the cold, gray sky.

That evening we sat around camp, eating instant mashed potatoes and hot dogs—our staple on all three hunts, which by this time we were getting a little tired of. We'd been snowed on a few times during the last sheep hunt, but as the sun set, the weather looked about as nice as it could get for September in the Interior. Shadows swept across valleys, the sun bathed hills in golden light, and distant snow-covered mountains jutted like carnivorous teeth into the blue horizon. We talked of caribou and how lucky we were to be in their country and able to hunt them. Though we were all meat hunters, Luke wanted a wall hanger and claimed he was going to pass on any small bulls for at least the first day. Reid was hoping for a freezer trophy: a young, tender, delicious bull. I was resolved to act only as a meat packer—my freezer was already getting pretty full of fresh salmon, venison, and a sheep.

"Caribou!" Reid hissed. My brothers quivered as a herd of a dozen massive bulls filed through the yellow, willow-covered valley below. A couple had bloody strips of velvet hanging from their three-foot-high splayed antlers. A group of cows and calves climbed toward a plateau. All moved steadily to the northwest—they could be thirty miles away by the following morning.

Before dawn, I awoke to the beautiful and eerie howling of a wolf from the valley. Soon the wind picked up, and snow began hissing against the walls of our tents. Luke and I crawled out into a blizzard just before dawn. We turned our backs to the weather, boiled a quick cup of tea, and set off in the direction the caribou had been moving the night before. Soon we were engulfed in a whiteout and plastered in wet snow. We could have been walking by whole herds. We were following a network of caribou trails through the gray when Luke fell to a crouch. Kneeling on a snowy tussock, I stared over his shoulder and saw a group of young bulls moving parallel to us through the storm. They were all perfect, the sort of animals I prefer harvesting for maximum taste and tenderness, but there were no massive bulls. A male caribou usually reaches maturity around six or seven years—no small feat considering that everything loves eating them. One bull was larger than the rest; Luke looked back at me and asked in a whisper what I thought.

"You've wanted a caribou rack for the wall for a long time," I said.

"This is so weird," Luke said. "I've never passed on an animal like that."

We trudged on in the direction where the big bulls had been heading the night before. A herd of cows and calves wended in and out of willow thickets in the valley below as the weather cleared. We clambered up to the top of a plateau where the icy wind blew fierce. Shale-covered mountains dusted with snow rose to the west and the north. Any other species would seek cover, but not caribou. The colder the weather, the happier they seem. A herd of two dozen milled on a nearby plateau. Luke and I down climbed until we were out of sight and used a series of ravines to make a stalk. With our hearts thundering, we peered over the edge and studied cows, calves, and subadult bulls. We moved on, taking time to glass each bowl and valley. Caribou would emerge from the tundra and mountains like magic, but none were adult bulls.

In the early afternoon, we sat in a barren saddle twelve miles from where we'd left the truck. This area had always been good to us during past hunts, but both of us were questioning the rationale behind hauling a bull so far from the road, especially when we'd encountered the herd of subadult males near camp. Luke was second-guessing his decision not to shoot when I saw the red flash of antlers in the willows a half mile away.

"There's your animal," I said, squinting through my scope. Two adult bulls, amidst a dozen cows and subadults, fed and thrashed through a willow thicket. We clambered down a steep ravine for coverage. Luke tumbled and smashed his left hand. His trigger finger swelled up so badly we wondered if it was broken. He shook it off and kept going. By the time we got within view of the herd, they were moving away, up into the mountains.

"Looks like they're gone," Luke said.

"Leave your pack with me," I said. "I bet you can get within range."

Witnessing Luke making a stalk is a bit awe inspiring. I have trouble walking up a mountain, but Luke is able to run without breaking a sweat. In a blizzard, he disappeared out of view, taking a direction he hoped would allow him to cut the herd off. By the time he was at the same elevation, I was feeling a little bad for encouraging him on a wild caribou chase. He belly crawled through snow to the

Luke and me with a nice bull taken in the mountains of the Fortymile country.

draw he was hoping the animals were following; I waved my jacket over my head and signaled the caribou were further away. By now the herd knew something was up, and the alpha cow was steadily leading the rest higher up the mountain. A moment later, a flock of ptarmigan, in their white winter plumage, exploded into flight at the hooves of the cow. Startled, she ran in the opposite direction, toward Luke. The two big bulls, twice the size of every other caribou, followed. When Luke saw antlers bobbing against the horizon, he stripped off his shirt for a rifle rest. My first thought was, *Damn, he's even whiter than a halibut's belly*, but as minutes elapsed, I began wondering how long it was possible to lie half naked in a blizzard without becoming hypothermic. At the crack of the shot, one of bulls keeled over. Twenty minutes later, sweating and out of breath, I climbed to the bench where Luke sat shivering next to a magnificent caribou. I passed him a couple jackets and gradually he warmed up.

"What a beautiful animal," I said, resting my hand on its warm body. For more than a half decade, the bull had wandered the Interior wilderness, hunted by wolves and people. He'd survived weeks of negative-sixty-degree temperatures during the winters and hordes of biting insects during the summer. He was an expression of the land itself. He was perfect.

"Thank you, God; thank you, caribou," Luke said. We butchered and began the long haul out. Late in the day, we encountered Reid hiking across a tussock field. He relieved us of a significant amount of meat, and together we busted through a valley of willows and climbed up to the top of a plateau. Still six miles from the road, without enough time to get out before dark, we buried the meat in a rock pile. We sat nearby, enjoying a peaceful evening and the pleasant scenery. Reid regaled us with a story of a bull moose he'd encountered; it had antlers wide enough to lie down in. Moose season opened the next day. Thankfully, none of us had a tag.

"This couldn't get any better," Reid said, watching the sun glow on the tundra.

"Yeah. Unless that young bull you were hoping to get ran by right now," Luke said. Less than a minute later, the clacking of tendons and thunder of hooves startled us.

"You got to be kidding," I said, as three young bulls stopped forty yards away and stared. Luke and I began laughing, but Reid was all business. He grabbed his rifle and in a few seconds assured that he'd have delicious eating for the year to come.

"He's exactly what I was hoping for," Reid said, kneeling over the caribou. We gutted him then broke his brisket and pelvis, propping open the rib cage with a stick so he would cool quickly. After covering the caribou in spruce boughs, we hiked across the darkening tundra toward camp. Scattered groups of caribou slowly came in and out of view along ridges and plateaus. That night we feasted on heart and instant mashed potatoes. Tomorrow would be a brutal pack out, but a few hours of pain for a winter of good eating is a pretty good deal.

BIRD DOG

MANY DOG OWNERS SUFFER from a syndrome in which they believe their pooch, even if it's yapping, narcissistic, and craps in the house, is nothing short of the canine messiah. I can't recall how many owners I've heard say, "Argos, Balto, and Ol' Yeller were all right, but they pale in comparison to my Fluffy Buns" as their little furball alternated between humping my foot and peeing on the rug. I'm fine with foot humping, but there's only so much urine a man can take on his rug. My older brother, Luke, cut to the heart of the matter.

"You're just not a dog guy," he told me.

"I had a dog, and that was good enough for me," I said referring to Buff, a yellow Lab I grew up with. Argos, Balto, and Ol' Yeller were all right, but Buff was the best of canines. Never mind if he incessantly barked, whined, fought, thieved, and had irreconcilable mama issues. My favorite part of being a teenager was running around in the woods with him. Reid, my little brother, loved that dog so much that the only art he put up in his house years later were photos of Buff. When it came to hunting, whether it was waterfowl or sooty grouse, Buff was a phenomenal retriever. I didn't see the point of getting another dog as none could compare.

Reid wasn't as hard edged. He searched out different breeders looking for Buff's doppelganger. He found a kennel in Anchorage that bred stocky, deep-chested English labs with big heads. He and his wife Meghan picked out Dory, a sweet little polar bear of a puppy, when she wasn't quite eight weeks. Right around then, my gal, MC, threatened to leave or maim me if we didn't get a dog. She'd spent the last year and a half searching the local pound and even tried to steal a few dogs that belonged to good homes. For some reason, getting a dog, even a rescue dog, in our hometown of Juneau is really hard. We were on the verge of signing up for a puppy from a litter of rescue feral mongrels—you know, the type that is half cat, half coyote, and a third rat—when we learned we'd be number sixty-seven on the waiting list if we passed the interview, background check, and a forty-page examination. With all the dog I ate in Cambodia and Vietnam a few years back, we both knew we had no chance. MC started screaming and breaking expensive china.

"Dammit, I'm buying a guinea pig, and I'll pretend it's a dog!" she yelled as she shattered a plate against the wall. "I just want something to pet and love!"

When our friends Jesse and Monika Walker decided to breed their golden retriever Pancho—a dog MC held in such high regard she had a picture of her and him on a walk together up on the wall—and promised us a pup, it felt like divine intervention. Reid and Luke cautioned me about getting a golden retriever, though.

"They're too pretty to be good bird dogs," Reid said.

"Might as well buy a condo, get a real job, and throw in the towel if you get a golden," Luke said. "They're easy, but I've never met one with much personality or intelligence."

I'd never seen MC so happy, so I knew my fate was sealed. When the puppies were four weeks, we had to choose between three. There was something about the female runt that struck me right from the get-go. MC felt the same way, so we called dibs on her. We named her Fenrir, who in Norse mythology was the wolf that killed Odin and destroyed the Earth, and called her Fen for short. Dory was a full-grown pup when she met eight-week-old Fen, but the two quickly became best friends. At first Dory would squash and toss Fen around like a little rag doll, but our tiny gal showed a propensity

Fenrir takes a break while floating the Big Salmon and Yukon Rivers.

for ferocity, often leaving her giant buddy with a bloody snout. Reid believed there wasn't a chance she'd turn into a bird dog, but he still offered his library on training a retriever.

"Thanks, but I think I'm going to take the Montessori School approach," I said. "I don't care if she becomes a bird dog as long as she's sweet."

Which was mostly true, but there was definitely a part of me that dreamed of Fen becoming my spring sooty grouse hunting partner.

A few weeks after we brought Fenrir home, she got her first real dose of the woods. With MC, my dad, and his blue heeler Loki, we drove from Skagway into the Yukon to float the Big Salmon River. Fen was a little unsure at first, but by day two she was living up to her namesake. One evening we sat for hours as a large pack of wolves howled nearby. We went to bed beneath a canopy of stars with Fen curled up between me and MC. Deep in the night, I woke to the sound of something creeping up on our tent.

"Get me the headlamp!" I said to MC. I grabbed my short barrel shotgun and was halfway out of the tent, prepared to sacrifice my-self to the jaws of a grizzly or horny whims of a Sasquatch for my dog and woman, when MC muttered in a not-so-pleasant voice.

"Get it yourself."

"What?" I glanced into the darkness of the tent and then back outside. Fenrir stirred a little in annoyance.

"It's hanging up," MC said again and then fell back asleep. I grabbed the light and crawled outside. In the morning, I made sure to point out the fresh wolf tracks and scat around our tents, but neither MC, Dad, or Fen seemed impressed. By the end of the trip, Fenrir had become the sort of dog that would have inspired Jack London to write a sequel to *The Call of the Wild*.

My brothers kept saying Fenrir would never retrieve. When I told them she'd be the best hunting dog they'd ever known (after Buff), they scoffed.

"You're not even training her," Reid said.

Over the winter, as Fen grew, I took her deeper into the woods and mountains. It soon became apparent she was going to be perhaps the smallest golden retriever I'd ever known. What my little brother didn't understand was that Fen and I had a relationship like Mr. Miyagi and Daniel-san. Making Fenrir do martial art poses on the bow of my canoe might not seem as practical as throwing dummies wrapped in feathers, but it worked out pretty well in the movie *The Karate Kid*. Reid was so adamant Fen wouldn't become a bird dog that we made a bet. If she didn't retrieve, I'd give him my left thumb, preserved in a jar of alcohol, for dinner party conversations. If she did, I could name his and Meghan's second child.

In April, when the booming of sooty grouse filled the mountains around Juneau, I put a scope on my old .22 rifle. I hadn't used the gun since Buff's last hunts more than ten years before. I walked into the woods not sure of how the day would go. Fen ran back and forth along deer trails and sniffed wolf hair as we hiked up a steep hill toward the hooting of a grouse. Occasionally, she would check in with me with a quick touch of her nose on my hand. The hooting of the grouse grew louder and deeper as I neared a giant spruce tree at the edge of an avalanche path. I found the grouse in the maze of branches and took a rest, and the bird came tumbling to the earth.

"Go get it!" I yelled, and Fen tore down the hill. The bird jumped up running and tried to fly with a broken wing. To my astonishment, my tiny golden retriever pounced, pinned it to a boulder, and without my saying anything, brought the very much alive bird back and placed it in my hands. Maybe it was a fluke—but the next hunt, she retrieved a bird Luke shot without any fuss. A few days later, Reid and I hiked up a mountain we'd hunted since we were kids. Dory and Fen wrestled as we followed an old hunter's trail high into towering jungle. We climbed past a waterfall and were able to hear a few grouse hooting on a ridge. Reid shot the first bird and mumbled a quiet acknowledgment when Fen brought it back and dropped it at his feet.

MC came on the next hunt. We hiked up an avalanche chute to a cliff and then traversed over and down onto a hooting grouse. She made a great shot, and a minute later, Fen brought her dinner. The next grouse spooked and got quiet before we could figure out what tree it was in. It took some time, but I found it perched on a branch. MC made a good shot, but the bird was able to glide away without us seeing where it landed. This sort of circumstance is when having a good hunting dog makes the difference between finding the bird and going home feeling bad. Fen and I followed a deer trail across the steep hill side and looked for feathers

"Got get it," I said, trying to encourage her to work the area. She was still just a pup at ten months. She looked at me confused for a few moments and then took off. When we were about two hundred yards from the tree the grouse had been perched in, Fen appeared with the bird. While we sat waiting for MC to catch up, I remembered adventures and hunts Buff and I'd shared. Fen stared up at me happily panting. For a few moments, I had something like déjà vu. MC arrived and then admired the bird for a while before cleaning and skinning it.

As we hiked home, we debated what to have for dinner. We agreed tonight it'd be grouse and potatoes. Tomorrow we'd have MC's favorite, grouse stew that she'd let simmer in the crockpot all day. That matter settled, I considered a good name for Reid and Meghan's next kid.

"How does Ruger Olaf Dihle sound?" I asked MC. She sighed, petted Fenrir, and continued on through a maze of devil's club toward the ocean.

THE FISH THAT REFUSED
TO GET AWAY

Note to the Reader: This essay is controversial and may lead to fish fights, hurt feelings, and even the end of a few friendships. The subject has long been an inflammatory and polarizing issue amongst anglers. Hopefully this will open diplomatic talks, and eventually some of us won't have to live in fear and shame for catching, and even eating, humpies.

PINK SALMON, even though they have a really cool scientific name (*Humpy*), aren't generally held in high esteem by fishermen. When the subject is broached in northern Southeast Alaska, folks generally shake their heads in disgust and say they don't eat bait. I've eaten my share of herring, worms, grasshoppers, and other insects—both to try to impress girls and because I frequently forget to pack a lunch—and feel it's my duty to defend the smallest and most abundant of the Pacific salmon. Let it be known: humpies are much tastier than bugs, worms, and herring. I didn't always feel this way. My history with humpies was much like that of many snobby Alaskan kids raised with ample amounts of delicious seafood.

It began with tormenting spawning humpies as soon as I could walk. I had little appreciation for the magnitude of the journey they'd made and the incredible thousand-to-one odds each fish had beat to spawn. In my defense, I was suffering from a mostly unknown sickness I call msihpromoporhtna, the opposite of anthropomorphism, where people, most often children, take on the characteristics of wild animals. I thought I was a bear and spent much time chasing, catching, and pretending to devour half-dead salmon. My parents struggled to get me to leave rotting salmon alone for years.

"You're never going to get a girlfriend smelling like spawned salmon!" my mom yelled at me all through high school. Sadly, I think msihpromoporhtna may be genetic, as my niece Braith used to spend hours in the pouring rain and wind dressed up as a sage grouse or donkey, howling and yipping like a coyote.

Eventually I overcame my species confusion and learned to catch fish with a pole and hook. Eager to fit in, I soon ran with the wrong fishermen, smoking, drinking, and badmouthing certain species of fish, mostly humpies. The following incident with a crab boat captain I deckhanded for illustrates my behavior during this period.

"I'd rather eat dirt than a humpy," the captain said, sizing me up as we chopped humpies into crab bait. He spat a huge glob of chewing tobacco onto a pile of rotting lumber.

"I'd rather eat crap than a humpy," I said, trying to spit juices from my grape-flavored bubble gum. He raised a bushy eyebrow and thought for a moment or two.

"I'd rather eat garbage than a humpy."

"I'd rather eat tofu than a humpy," I said.

"Ah, you're a true fisherman!" He slid another half dozen humpies onto the piece of plywood I was using as a cutting board.

A few years later, when I began to explore and fish Cross Sound, I met battle-scarred fishermen so haunted by humpies they had trouble sleeping at night. In the 1970s and 1980s, much of the Cross Sound trolling fleet made their bread, diesel, and beer off fishing humpies. It was a fishery that made you feel like Conan the Barbarian in a zombie apocalypse movie. After a successful day, the boat and fishermen were covered in slime, blood, and scales. A season or two of doing this and people began to get arthritis and tendonitis from repeating the same motions of clipping gear, landing fish, and popping hooks.

Joe Craig, a veteran Cross Sound captain I worked for, made no effort to hide his feelings for humpies.

"We're not fishing for them. Other folks might keep them, and sure it adds up, but I will not allow a humpy aboard this vessel," he said, and then he stared out onto the slate-gray ocean. I heard rumors of a hotline being set up for trollers suffering from post-traumatic-humpy-fishing disorder.

For the big July 1 king salmon opener, Joe and I trolled along the outer coast through pea-soup fog. The humpies were thick, so I was busy on the gurdies hauling in lines and shaking them off so a king or coho might take their place. I didn't keep a tally, but I'm pretty sure we were catching more than five hundred some of those days. On the third or fourth day out, I shook a small humpy from a hoochie and watched it plop into the frothing ocean then strike the next spoon coming up on the trolling line. Befuddled, I lifted it out of the water and released it again. The fish hovered near the next spoon, and suddenly I felt strangely inspired.

"Damn the hook, go for it!" I yelled.

"What?" Joe called from the cabin over the diesel engine.

"Oh, just got a humpy here that's refusing to get away."

"Absolutely no humpies allowed aboard!"

I shrugged at the fish, and it disappeared into the depths. Staring at the foam and sloshing waves, something changed in me. I might be too snobby to eat a humpy, but here was a fish whose tenacity I had to respect. Thus inspired, two months later, when I had access to the Internet, I looked up some information on them.

Apparently pink salmon get their name from the color of their flesh, not because they are the most feminine of the salmon, which was what I always believed. I learned that *humpy* is actually a nickname, not a scientific designation, and it comes from the hump that forms on males a while before they find a stream, tide pool, or bucket to spawn in. All along I thought the name humpy came from their fecundity; no longer can I call them the bunnies of the sea. They have a life cycle of two years, so even- and odd-year schools are said to possess different genetics. Most often they return to the same stream they hatched from. Lost, small schools of pinks are known to colonize streams that have formed after glaciers have receded from the land. Not only do they feed people, bears, birds, and a host of other creatures, their rotting carcasses add nutrients to the soil and are partially responsible for how ridiculously brushy and miserable the country surrounding most salmon streams is.

Armed with this knowledge and an open mind, I began an odyssey that eventually led me back to the spawning grounds I once terrorized. First under the guidance of my older brother, Luke, and two of his daughters, Adella and Braith, I found myself, pole in hand, watching pink salmon darken the water. A slight drizzle fell from shape-shifting clouds. The ocean lapped towards the jungley forest rising into the mist. The first cast, though it yielded no hits, felt like absolution. Adella, seven years old, took charge with a quarter-ounce pixie, flinging it like an expert to where a fish had just finned the surface.

"Got one," she said calmly a few casts later. I dropped my pole onto the beach and ran over to not miss the action.

"Is it a big one?" I asked.

"She won't know until she gets it in closer," Braith, five years old, explained. Adella played the fish perfectly, adjusting her reel's drag to complement the fish when it ran.

"Can we keep it?" I asked when she had the fish near the shore.

"Nope, it's too dark," Adella said, and then she added, "The tide is taking your pole away."

I hustled back to grab my pole. Before I had time to lose my lure to the rock it had snagged on, Adella had another fish on. She took after her mother, Trish, whose hands were prophetic when a fishing rod was placed in them. Braith stuck with her dad, reeling in fish until she got tired. Then Adella would make me reel in her line so she could help her little sister bring her catch in. Eventually, they had a few silver pinks on the beach, and the girls asked for knives. They'd forgotten their own at home. Kneeling next to the ocean's edge, they gutted fish, saving the eggs to feed their chickens. When I pulled out my camera, Braith made her best dead salmon face and Adella smiled thoughtfully. Though I couldn't help feel we were bringing home bait, everyone agreed the humpy cakes we ate that night tasted good.

A week later, I was sitting with MC on the shore of Seymour Canal on Admiralty Island watching pink salmon jump continuously. In

Adella guts a pinks salmon.

the last hour or so, while we were beachcombing, a brown bear had dropped a fresh humpy, minus a large bite, next to our kayak. For a few minutes, we sat in awe of the flood of life until the crackling of brush let us know the bear was watching nearby.

"We're sorry. We're leaving," we called, jamming our gear in the hatches of our kayak.

The current carried us past multitudes of leaping salmon of different sizes and coloration. In the distance, numerous eagles and a large brown bear crowded the mouth of a salmon stream teeming with a mixture of pink and chum salmon. A few large, uniformly dark salmon jumped, making me wonder if some kings were spawning in the stream as well. The bear slowly moved upstream, erupting a flock of Bonaparte gulls into a white fury. We bobbed with the waves, watching schools of salmon wait for the tide to rise so they could swim upstream. Close to the mouth of the stream, the ocean roiled to life with thousands of fleeing humpies.

"I'm sorry for neglecting and mistreating you," I said quietly.

"I forgive you," MC said and then lit up. "Just try to remember to cut your toenails. Have you seen how many scars I have? And only you think your jokes are funny. They're really just childish. And shower more often; you smell like a spawned salmon."

"I was apologizing to the humpies that haunt me," I mumbled. There was a long pause, only interrupted by the shrieking of the gulls and the splashing of salmon.

"Salmon sure are amazing," MC said. It was a slow and silent paddle back to camp.

FROM FOREST
TO FREEZER

THE GREEN MOUNTAINS of Admiralty Island rose into the blue sky. It was August, my favorite month, when fat bucks are high in the mountains, the sea is full of salmon, and Southeast Alaskan freezers are most easily filled. My friend Dennis Hall and I hauled an inflatable boat past a bear's bed just inside the guard timber. A dozen pried-open cockle clam shells lay nearby, and the smell of rotting salmon hung in the air. We hoisted our boat and excess gear high in a tree and followed a heavily used bear trail up a ridge. The sun quickly set as we climbed past Sitka spruce and western hemlock trees, their branches adorned with old man's beard moss. By the light of headlamps, we pitched a tent on a small bench.

Dawn was beginning to illuminate the Coast Mountains and the Juneau Icefield when we made it to alpine the following morning. Seymour Canal and Stephens Passage stretched glassy and pink below. Two does watched us skeptically before vanishing into brush. The hooves and hides of three bucks killed by other hunters lay along the top of the mountain. A bear had torn up the earth and buried the remains. Deep indentions in the earth showed where bears had walked the same path for generations. We split up to cover more ground; in the hours afterward, I'd counted six does and fawns and a buck that flashed through an opening seven hundred yards away. I circled around but knew there was little chance of seeing him again. At noon I found Dennis asleep at the top of the mountain. It was too hot, so I sprawled out and took a nap too. The sky began to cloud and the temperature dropped.

"There ought to be some bucks moving around," Dennis said as we hunted our way back toward tree line. Late in the evening, Dennis found a good vantage to post up. I hiked a few hundred yards away to scope a big valley. I was preparing to go home skunked when a deer appeared atop a cliff. Not knowing if it was a doe or buck, I waited for it to step out of view and then made a rapid stalk. I lay behind a jack pine, calming my heart until the deer stepped out. A quick look through the scope showed a wide set of antlers. I worked the bolt, took a breath, and judging my rest solid, pulled the trigger when the buck turned broadside. He tumbled into a maze of five-foot-high ferns, thrashed for a few seconds, and then lay still. I thanked him and set to field dressing so we'd be able to get the meat in a good position to haul out the following morning. Dennis, hearing the shot, hiked over and showed me his preferred manner to butcher. Instead of gutting the animal, we started on an outer side. He worked on a hindquarter while I sliced off the shoulder, neck meat, rib scraps, and one backstrap. Dennis reached under and cut free the tenderloin before we flipped the deer over and started on the other side. After harvesting every usable bit of meat and loading it into our packs, I slowly followed my friend up a steep and slippery slope to the top of a ridge. It was dark by the time we stashed the meat in stunted mountain hemlock trees. I kept the game bags off the ground so the meat would cool and ermine, shrews, and mice would have a harder time getting into it. There was a chance I'd lose the meat to a bear, a risk hunters face when there aren't suitable trees to get meat high off the ground. I positioned the cache so I would be able to see it from a distance. We made camp upwind, a hundred or so yards away.

In the morning, a southerly blew thirty miles per hour, rain splattered against the tent, and a thick fog enveloped the mountain. I dumped a shrew out of my boot and cautiously approached the cache. I boned out all the quarters except for one ham on which I

Me with a Sitka blacktail in the mountains of Admiralty Island.

kept the evidence of sex attached. The shrew joined me as I sliced off copious amounts of fat. He ran over my leg onto a backstrap. The hike down through heavy fog took some route finding and occasional backtracking. At the beach, we dropped our packs, relieved to have the weight off. We paddled into wind and spray as the carcasses of spawned-out humpy salmon bobbed in the waves.

At home, hours later, I threw on dry clothes, put on a pot of tea, and set out three trays and a couple of cutting boards. My nine-week-old golden retriever puppy Fenrir lapped up puddles of blood on the kitchen floor then lay on my feet as I got to work. One tray was for roasts and steaks. One was for sausage. One was for jerky. Earlier that week, I'd turned a lot of the meat from two bucks into burger. The smell of meat, wild and rich, made me think of how lucky I was to be able to eat what the mountains and forest provide. I sliced up the heart and fried it for an early dinner. Soon all the roasts and steaks were in the freezer, positioned to maximize air flow to quicken freezing. A couple choice pieces I'd drop off for friends. The ribs would go to the family of a friend with three little kids who love a good, messy feed. I mixed in a marinade of spices and soy sauce for jerky and prepped the rest of the meat to make sausage the next day—I'd have to run by the grocery store to pick up some pig fat beforehand.

That night I lay in bed smelling like and thinking about deer. I remembered the mountains in the evening light and the calm ocean far below. I remembered the thrill of seeing the buck step out on the cliff. I remembered the stalk, the rapidity of movement over wet and slippery vegetation. I remembered the shot, the enormity of violence as the buck tumbled and died. I remembered his scent and warmth as he lay amidst the tall ferns. I remembered the hot blood and the subtle musk of his meat. Most of all I remembered my own gratefulness tinged with sadness as I sat with him, unsure if I was worthy of such a gift.

THE WOLF AND
THE FAWN

A FEW YEARS AGO while looking for deer, I listened to trees creaking and moaning in a Southeasterly gale. Snow fell steadily, illuminating the gloomy forest. I continued up a mountainside I planned to hunt and soon came across the fresh tracks of a wolf. The week before, I'd passed on three does in this area. Now, I jumped one big deer that was probably a buck. A few minutes after, I spied a big doe traversing a bench below. I watched her in my scope, imagining how good she would taste, but refrained from pulling the trigger.

I had taken my rifle for a lot of pleasant walks in the woods that December, but I was growing a little anxious. The season was almost over, and I could use one more buck. Between the weather and the wolf, my chance of eating fresh heart and backstrap for dinner was seeming pretty low. I'd hunted this mountainside a number of times and knew all the best benches and open stands of trees. So did the wolf. I half expected to bump into it.

I find encounters with megafauna in the rainforest more intense, intimate, and somehow special than out in the open. Whenever I see a deer in old growth, it feels like a small miracle. My brothers are quick to point out I feel this way because I don't

A wolf in the Brooks Range.

see that many. I've only seen one wolf, and just a fleeting glimpse, while deep in the forest. Another time, when I was kneeling over a freshly killed and partly eaten deer I'd found, wolves began howling nearby. I walked away, glancing over my shoulder. At the parking lot at the base of that trail, after stepping around McDonald's litter and a dirty diaper, I sat in my car wondering if I had tainted the kill for the wolves merely by discovering it.

The odds of running into the wolf were even worse than me shooting a buck. After a half hour of creeping along the mountainside and constantly running into its tracks, I admitted defeat. There was something almost hypnotic about the restless forest and the falling snow. I hunted in the opposite direction—even though the wind was poor—squinting in the hopes of seeing movement or the shape of an animal.

At dusk I still hadn't seen a deer. I began the hunter's walk of shame, one I know all too well, homeward. The screeching of ravens and eagles roused me from my doldrums. Soon I came across fresh tracks of the wolf, this time leading toward the avian ruckus. Though there was barely any light left, I circled upwind and began creeping closer. It was brushy and the snow was deep, but the storm masked most of my sound.

A fawn, partly covered in snow, lay fully intact near the base of a large jack pine. I knelt and brushed snow off. The birds must have only recently arrived, because her marble eyes were still intact.

I mentally cursed the wolf. It was silly to apply my sense of morality to nature, but killing and wasting a baby deer didn't sit well with me.

Something seemed odd, though. The fawn appeared to have died this morning. With how hard the snow was falling, the wolf's tracks couldn't be more than an hour old. I rubbed her fur and my hand came away covered in congealed blood. I parted the hair on her neck and jabbed my finger into a bullet hole. The shadows of ravens eyed me greedily and the blurs of eagles screeched with an excitement that bordered hysteria. They hopped from snowy bough to bough, flapped wildly, and glided in circles just above the stunted muskeg trees.

I sat with the fawn for a short while before whispering an apology and getting out my knife. I skinned out a tiny and still warm hindquarter and sliced it free from the spine. I sniffed the flesh, hoping to salvage what I could, but I was too late. The trees whispered and moaned as I hiked home. Soon even the sounds of the birds fighting and feasting faded into the storm.

THE TRAILS WE FOLLOW

WHEN I WAS KID I wanted to be a mountain man. Now I have a thirty-year mortgage, a pocket-sized golden retriever, and a gal who demands things as outlandish as an occasional conversation. I went to see the movie *The Revenant* with my older brother, Luke. It's about Hugh Glass, who got mauled by a grizzly and abandoned by his partners in the early 1800s. Reviewers claimed it was a brutal show of mansome savagery. After watching it, I heard others in the theater whispering they needed someone, anyone, to hold them gently and tell them it was all right. Luke and I were disturbed, too— not because of how brutal the movie was, but because it was a stark reminder of how soft we'd become. I went home, ate nachos, drank beer, and cried myself to sleep. Luke, on the other hand, decided to hike around Douglas Island. He tried to get me to join him, but I told him I didn't have time. The hike is thirty-some miles, with a little less than a third of it going through the woods and over cliffs. The rest of it is rocky beach. While he was hiking, encountering wolves, and doing other cool things, I sat staring at my computer and worrying about impending deadlines on a book and articles I was supposed to be writing. He showed up at my door thirteen hours or

Wolverine tracks on a glacier deep in the St. Elias Mountains.

so after he started—I live at the southern end of the road on Douglas Island—looking like he was just getting warmed up. I immediately launched into how tiring my day had been.

"Goldarn, I'm sure pooped from staring at my computer for the last twelve hours," I said, rising stiffly and throwing out my back when I bent to put on my boots before giving him a ride back to his car.

Since he'd seen wolves, I set a trail camera up on a point on the west side of the island. A week or so later, with Fenrir, my tiny golden retriever, I walked back to see if had I caught anything. A big pack had passed within yards, but none had triggered the camera. Nearby, a northern saw-whet owl was perched on an alder above the wolves' trail. I walked back quickly as I needed to shower before going to work—I smelled like the love child of Bigfoot and a skunk that ate spicy Thai food. The wolves' trail cut into the sodden maze of the rainforest. I tried to keep my dog close. My gal, MC, normally a cute little hippie chick, once told me if I ever let a wolf get Fenrir she wouldn't rest until she'd "hunted down, tortured, and killed them all."

"I mean, like, make wolves extinct!" she screamed, breaking a bottle of kombucha against the wall and smearing her face with organic hummus.

Perhaps it was the wolves, combined with the feeling I was spending too much time living artificially, that brought back memories of another wolf trail I encountered years ago. The February I was nineteen, I set out on a series of expeditions, hoping eventually to turn into a mountain man. The first trip was a ten-day slog into the woods, rivers, and mountains around Berners Bay. On the seventh day, I came upon the tracks of a wolf and a young moose. They weren't more than an hour or so old, and they followed the frozen Gilkey River toward a giant glacier. Blood lay in splatters every few yards. Mountains rose into a pale-blue sky; the snowy valley was silent except for my breath and the sound of my snowshoes. I followed for hours, hoping around every bend I'd come upon the wolf, its face covered in blood, standing above the steaming hulk of the moose. At dusk, storm clouds blotted out the mountains, and snow began to fall. Soon there was only darkness—by headlamp I plodded to a stand of giant Sitka spruce trees, built a fire, and made dinner as snow hissed and trees moaned.

Fenrir invested some wolf scat in yellow beach grass and, in two wags of her tail, swallowed a turd.

"You may be pretty," I scolded her, "but you're a sick puppy."

She lost interest in my lecture and went to sniff the tracks of a big deer. It had dragged its hooves and zigzagged nervously—having the wolves around must have been nothing short of terrifying for it. The previous fall, while floating a river, MC and I nearly had a moose jump into our small inflatable boat. Twenty minutes later, we'd encountered a pack of a dozen or so wolves. As the shadows lengthened, I wondered if the wolves were hunting right now. With warm winters, the deer had been fat and plentiful. I supposed I shouldn't resent the wolves for being what they are. After all, there were four deer, several halibut, and salmon in my freezer. They would help sustain me and my family through the year, and I'd given meat to several people who cherished it.

After the season, I'd cleaned my rifle, a 7mm Magnum my dad gave me for my sixteenth birthday. Through the years, I'd beaten the hell out of it chasing deer and mountain goats through the mountains and woods of my home in Southeast Alaska. When

I lived in Fairbanks, it accompanied me into the Brooks Range on hunts for caribou. Sometimes still, I bring it back to the Interior to chase caribou or sheep. It has a heavy trigger pull, one I'd grown so accustomed to that shooting other rifles felt unnatural. The stock needed to be refinished and the barrel reblued, to name a few repairs. My brothers, who both hunt with .338s, like to tease me it's a great rifle for ptarmigan and grouse.

I'd never told my brothers, but once, when I almost shot a brown bear with it, I wished for a heavier caliber. I was on a mountain on Admiralty Island and had just split up with my buddy Mike Janes when I heard the bushes moving nearby. Smiling to myself, I belly crawled toward a hummock for a rest on what I assumed would be a fat Sitka blacktail. I had no deer in the freezer yet. The previous winter, brutal and relentless with heavy snows, killed most. I'd shot a number of fat bucks at tree line in this area in years past, so I was expecting things to be routine. I gently chambered a bullet and waited for the deer to show. The mountain hemlock and jack pines shook like a freight train was passing through, and a brown bear, coal black in coloration, came charging out. It froze just twenty yards away. It kept one paw raised, and its mouth was frothing with foam and dripping with saliva. It glared with a bowel-liquefying intensity at the brush I'd quietly walked through just moments before. I put the crosshairs on its giant skull and tried to calm my rapidly beating heart. There was no question it was hunting, hoping to tear into a deer or perhaps another bear. A voice in my head calmly said, *Bjorn, if you don't kill that bear, it's going to kill you.*

After what felt like eons of watching the bear stare at the bushes I'd walked through, I pressed into the earth and slowly belly crawled backwards. When I was out of view, I rose and continued backing away, expecting the bear to come charging at any moment. I found Mike a short while later, sitting at the edge of a bowl and glassing.

"You mind if we hunt together?" I asked. Mike was understanding. We shot no deer that day, though we could have taken a few does. In the evening, shortly before we began our dash back to the ocean and the skiff, my friend gestured down at an open slope below.

"That your bear?" he asked. A large, black-colored bear swaggered across an avalanche path. I nodded. Mike is an understated man.

An aggressive Admiralty Island brown bear that Luke and I encountered during a long walk.

When he said, "That looks like a bad bear," I didn't disagree.

Before the 7mm Mag, my dad had lent me his father's old .308. I nearly broke it when I was being a fool and took a bad fall on a mountain. That gun likely saved my life when it got hung up in a jack pine and kept me from taking a very long tumble off a cliff. My dad never said anything other than "It seems someone is looking out for you." He put the rifle away in closet, where it has remained untouched for nearly two decades. I should bring it to a gunsmith someday. It shoots true despite its injuries and malfunctioning bolt. It would be a great rifle to pass on to a kid.

When I'd finished cleaning my rifle, the smell of deer mixed with gun oil on my hands, I put it away in the closet. I leaned it next to an ancient shotgun that my good friend Joe Craig, with whom I had commercial fished with for a number of years, had given me a few months before he passed on. I'd killed a few grouse with it, pulled down on a giant brownie high on a forested mountain on Chichagof Island that rose to its full height out of the gloom at spitting distance. Later that summer, on Yakobi Island, I covered an angry sow with it as she was trying to decide whether or not to try to tear into me. Next to Joe's shotgun was the 12 gauge I bought when I was fourteen or fifteen. It's by far suffered the most abuse. I used it for protection on Admiralty and Chichagof for more than a decade and encountered dozens of bears, often quite close, but I had never once pointed it at one. I ran my fingers over their barrels. My shotgun was still oiled from the fall when I was wandering up salmon streams. Joe's gun was coated with dust. I wiped the barrel clean with a cloth, slid the closet door shut, and said goodbye to the season.

It occurred to me, as Fenrir waited at the end of the trail that day on Douglas, that I was smiling and lost in memories. The woods lit up with the golden light that comes right before the sun sets. I'd forgotten about all the things I was supposed to be stressing over and instead was planning new adventures and hunts I hoped to make. I drove home thinking how wolves, stress, caribou, domestic paradoxes, money, alcoholism, fear, hate, friendship...how everything leaves a trail to follow. The paths we choose, or are placed on and can't figure out how to get off of, end up defining our lives. We don't always realize the journey we've taken until we're at the trail's end. Right when I thought I was getting deep, Fenrir vomited in my lap. Apparently wolf shit doesn't stay down that easily.

"Well, princess, I hope you learned your lesson," I said, petting my dog. We drove through the darkness. I may have become fat, pathetic, and bland, but I knew, in a way, I'd always be traveling over a frozen river chasing the tracks and blood of a moose and wolf, hoping to catch up.

IN THE TIME OF PTARMIGAN

I USED TO HUNT PTARMIGAN fairly often, even relying on the birds for food during long, solitary wanders. The last one I shot was nearly a decade ago, though. It happened during a deer hunt on Lincoln Island when stormy seas inspired me and my brothers to spend the night out in the pouring rain without gear or food. We cooked the bird along with a coho over a fire in a skunk cabbage-roofed lean-to we'd built.

There's not a lot of meat on any of the three species of ptarmigan. The largest, the willow ptarmigan, offers enough for a solitary meal. The meat is dark and tasty, though I've heard some people say they find it a little gamy. Classified as arctic grouse, their feathers change from white during snowy months to varying earthen shades during warmer months.

When I was twenty, I abandoned college for the mountains, and ptarmigan became a significant part of my life. My older brother, Luke, reluctantly drove me out the Steese Highway, northeast of Fairbanks.

"No booze, no ice cream, no chili con queso, no Kentucky Fried Chicken." I was listing all I was giving up when a low-flying ruffed grouse brained itself on the bumper.

"Well, I imagined bagging my first ruff to be a little different," Luke said as he gutted the bird. He'd just moved to Fairbanks from Southeast and was eager to explore the new hunting opportunities. We spent half a day trying to jump grouse to no avail. Luke walked to the truck, and I headed toward the mountains. I set up my tent on a high alpine ridge then sat for a while trying to meditate and have deep thoughts. The croaking of rock ptarmigan disrupted my thoughts of pizza, booze, and girls. A half dozen birds whose plumage had recently turned white in preparation for winter glided across a ridge and set down. As stealthily as I could, I crawled within ten yards and then proceeded to empty my recently purchased Henry Survival .22 rifle. The birds eyed me somewhat irritably. Finally, a bullet must have ricocheted, or perhaps one had a heart attack, because a bird fell over.

I was crouched over a pot of boiling ptarmigan soup when I suddenly sensed that a large presence had snuck up and was watching me. My thoughts flashed to the fresh tracks of a grizzly I'd stumbled upon a game trail in the brush earlier that day. Slowly, I looked up. A young bull caribou stood just yards away.

The caribou and I studied each other for a half minute before it limped down a shale-covered slope, utilizing trails etched into the mountain by other caribou, Dall sheep, and wolves. The sun set behind the Crazy Mountains, a series of hills rising out of the monotony of the taiga to the north, as I drank broth and felt the energy of the earthy-tasting flesh transfer into me.

I followed wolf tracks through fresh snow along a ridge, above a one-thousand-foot vertical granite wall. A small herd of Dall sheep lay nestled in the lee of the wind. I stalked croaking ptarmigan and happily filled my dinner pot.

Two days later, while walking across an expanse of tussocks, a caribou appeared on the tundra's horizon. It ran toward me, its gangly gait arrested by a slight limp, until it was twenty feet away. The animal appeared to be the young bull from two evenings before, that or his doppelganger. It looked at me for a few moments and then began browsing lichens and willows.

I scanned the area for wolves and bears before looking back to the caribou. I yelled. Failing to have any effect, I flung handfuls of earth at the young bull. He took a few steps away and looked at me with confusion. I yelled, "I'm a man! You're a caribou! You need to fear me!" and then walked rapidly away. A few moments later, the caribou caught up and kept pace. An hour later, a dozen caribou appeared about three hundred yards away. My unexpected traveling partner had yet to leave my side.

"Look there," I said, gesturing at the small herd. "Caribou. Your friends."

One bull was quite large, his naked antlers towering well over three feet above his head. I dropped my pack at the edge of a small pool and began the slow process of filtering drinking water. The young caribou walked to the other side of the pool and began grazing just feet away.

"Caribou, over there," I said again and pointed. He looked at me before going back to eating. I ate a granola bar, which did little to satiate my hunger. I did not have much food and still had a long way to go. For a few moments, I fantasized about killing him and how delicious he'd taste roasted over a fire. It was so bad I began to drool.

"I'm sorry. You're the only friend I have." He looked at me. My words and their stupidity felt so alien I didn't speak again for days. I ate another granola bar, and we traveled on. Hours later, in the deep evening, he began wandering farther away. On occasion he disappeared behind a knoll or hill for a few minutes and then came running back. Shortly before I stopped to make camp, as the blood-red orb of the sun crept low on the horizon, he vanished into the gloomy tundra. A flock of fifty or so shimmering white ptarmigan flew overhead and landed a few hundred yards away. It was my first chance of the day to fill my cook pot, so I made a stalk and killed two. The fading warmth of their bodies temporarily eased the cold in my hands. Another large flock flew past, the sound of their wings momentarily breaking the heavy silence. I removed only the intestines and feathers, and boiled the rest of the birds as the sun disappeared behind the mountains. Storm clouds told of a blizzard that would soon come. I scanned the tundra until dark, hoping the caribou would reappear.

It grew colder and darker, and my food supplies dwindled with each passing day. Half-starved ptarmigan hunting with a misfiring, free-thinking, anti-survival .22 led to some frustrations. A couple times, I put down my gun and picked up rocks. When a bullet struck home, a sort of happiness, akin to winning the lottery, came over me. Sitting on a tussock in an expanse of tundra or on a rock high in the mountains, chewing dark chunks of willow and rock ptarmigan meat and drinking life-giving broth, I became renewed. At my last camp, before returning to the Steese Highway, the sound of hooves clacking and vegetation being chewed woke me in the morning. With a strange mixture of admiration and hunger, I watched a nice bull caribou grazing nearby.

A few days after I'd hitchhiked back to Fairbanks, Luke, hoping to harvest a berry-fed black bear, agreed to drop me off on another slog. We trudged up a drainage, past an inquisitive red fox and a cow moose browsing red and yellow willows. From atop an icy plateau, the white mountains and glaciers of the eastern Alaskan Range rose into an ominously dark sky.

"You sure you want to go in there?" Luke asked the following morning as we broke camp. I nodded, and we said our goodbyes. Two moose working the edge of the plateau paused from their browsing to eye me as I crunched through snow and blazing-red willow. Three big bull caribou ran in circles, trying to get my scent in the calm afternoon. Near the terminus of a glacier, a small flock of white-tailed ptarmigan blended in nearly perfectly with the snowy landscape. The smallest and rarest of the three species of ptarmigan, they're not known to exist north of the Alaska Range. Being a wildlife nerd, I was familiar with the characteristics of each of the three species of ptarmigan. Inspired by an almost constant hunger, I created my own criteria based off my belly for classification. White-tailed ptarmigan, inhabiting high alpine and glacial moraine, equaled two to three to fill belly. Rock ptarmigan, preferring more moderate mountainous terrain, equaled two to fill belly. Willow ptarmigan, lovers of bands of willows and tundra, equaled one for satiated belly, two for stuffed belly.

The days passed in a steady procession of ridge walking and stirring vistas. Occasionally, I'd get to the top of something, scratch my butt, and hope to feel something a little more profound than being tired, hungry, and lonely. There were scatterings of caribou, fresh

A willow ptarmigan at the northern limit of the Brooks Range.

sheep, and fresh wolf sign, and coveys of white-tailed ptarmigan near glaciers that I ate a couple of each night. One night the aurora encompassed most of the sky in a wriggling mass of purples, greens, and reds.

The following morning, I woke well before dawn and hiked toward a distant mountain. A cow caribou, her breath steaming in the gloom, danced circles around me as the sun slowly edged the eastern horizon. The first river I crossed was hidden beneath a thick layer of ice. A few hours later, I traversed a glacier and followed a narrow ridge that looked like it would lead to a glaciated slope and then the summit. I was about an hour or less away from the top when I became aware of a butt so big and jiggly it would make Kim Kardashian envious bouncing its way up the ridge. The sun was in my eyes, and my first thought was, *Goldarn, that's a big marmot.* With the summit on my mind and not wanting to waste another second, I put my head down and kept hiking. Soon, as plump and hairy butts often do in the wild, the rear end turned into a fairly irritated yet strikingly beautiful golden-red grizzly. The ridge was about to end in a steep, glaciated slope, and on both sides were near vertical cliffs.

My next thought was, *Shucks, it's going to be hard to get to the top now.* The bear refused to budge another inch. The hair on its hump and back stood up, and it glared to let me know it wasn't going to pick a fight but wasn't going to let me bully it either. My third thought was, *Wow, bear, you're a real weirdo for being up here on this mountain.*

I slowly backed away, heart pounding and ice ax clutched ready, even though I knew it was at best an inadequate defense. I descended the ridge, crossed the glacier, and though it was late, began trying to climb the peak via a more difficult route. The grizzly, a red dot on the other ridge, appeared frozen and watching for hours. Toward dusk, I turned around and cursed my luck for running into the bear. Preoccupied with these thoughts, I walked into a small herd of Dall sheep. A large ram eyed me warily before leading the group away. In darkness, by the light of the moon, I followed the fresh tracks of wolves back to my tent.

Winter came the next day and shut down my last attempt on another summit. That night as I sat in my tent, a real storm rolled in. A particularly strong gust of wind tore at my tent and then threw it into the sky. After a flip or two, I slammed atop a boulder and snapped two out of three tent poles. I undid the third, rolled a number of big rocks inside the collapsed tent, and clung to a large boulder as the wind did its best to try to tear me away. Waking to deep silence, I undid the zipper and shoveled through a half foot of snow to be greeted with a much-appreciated blue sky. Bruised, happy, and tired, I began the two-day slog back to the highway. I hitched a ride to Fairbanks with an old trapper from Eagle.

After a break of a few days, I hitched a ride with another trapper to Delta Junction then south to the Denali Highway. I snowshoed into the foothills south of the Hayes Range and wandered. In the ensuing three weeks, my food supplies dwindled, my stove stopped working, and I subsisted on frozen canola oil and ptarmigan. Unprepared for the harshness of minus forty temperatures, blizzards, and darkness, my two-month escapade ended with a fifty-hour slog down the Denali Highway. I froze my feet—and the tips of many other body parts—on the snowy road, losing any potential of becoming a respected explorer. Even better, at the edge of the Parks Highway, in a moment of blind exhaustion, I froze my tongue to my mountaineering snow shovel. I couldn't help but laugh—not an easy thing to do with a shovel hanging from my mouth. Doing my best to look natural, I climbed up to road's shoulder and stuck my thumb up. To my surprise, the first truck skidded to a stop. The driver swung the door open and smiled.

"Get in. Name's Mike. You look like a darn popsicle," he bellowed. He'd spent the last few days helping an older friend get his house together for the long winter and was now on his way back to Fairbanks. He looked and laughed like Chris Farley, immediately making me at ease. After spending three weeks without seeing or talking to anyone and feeling about as close to the void as I ever had, his company was a gift I'll never forget. He told stories of living in the bush: a black bear stalking his son when he was a toddler, his struggle to put enough food on the table during lean years, the beauty and versatility of white spruce versus the spindly black spruce, and much more. His optimistic philosophy on life no matter what fate served up was contagious. In the three and half hours we spent driving and talking, I felt I'd gained more perspective from his open kindness than I had in the two months wandering alone.

Mike dropped me off at the university, and I called my brother from a payphone. I huddled on a bench and waited. A pretty girl sat nearby doing her homework.

"You come back with any more sense?" my brother hollered as he walked up the stairs. Painfully, I rose and picked up my giant backpack. My backpack had had time to defrost, and a large pool of blood had formed on the floor where it had been resting. The girl gasped.

"It's okay!" I said holding up my hands, fingertips blistered and black with gangrene, to calm her. "It's only ptarmigan blood!"

OF RELATIONSHIPS
AND FREEZERS

I PURGE MY FREEZER once a year, whether I need to or not. This usually happens after my gal, MC, is unable to find room for something like a bag of vegetables and starts to rage. For instance, last July, after looking in the filled-to-the-brim freezer, she pulled out a frozen mountain goat femur and clubbed me over the head. When I came to, I'd been dragged into cave and was lying across a stone altar. She stood above me with a giant bear skull raised above her head.

"It's not normal to have your freezer full of bags of random animal parts!" she yelled.

"Most women would be happy to have salmon heads, bones, grouse wings, halibut carcasses, and a variety of skulls yet to be identified by science," I whined.

"The Paleolithic epoch is over!"

"Then why are you about to crush my head with a bear skull?" I asked. "Look at it this way, we have plenty of goodies for Halloween trick-or-treaters and Christmas stocking stuffers."

After I convinced her not to sacrifice me, I opened the freezer to find a motley collection of garbage bags. Most I didn't remember putting there. One looked ominous. A heavy dread tinged with

Me and MC with a nice halibut—every part of which I'll store in our freezer, as you never know when some halibut gonads will come in handy. (Photo courtesy of Nils Dihle)

excitement filled me. I half expected to find Jimmy Hoffa's head. I clawed through the plastic and took stock of a pile of frozen coho heads molded together. There were at least another half dozen similar mystery bags. It was time to face the truth. I suffered from an odd hoarding condition, one that is likely not treatable and leads to relationship strife.

A few days later, I headed out with my dad on his skiff and committed the contents of the bags to the sea. Sooty grouse wings floated away and made me bite my lip. Some poor kid just lost a great toy. As a ball of venison fat, sinew, and bloodshot meat sunk into the ocean, I considered singing the theme song for the movie *Titanic*, but my dad redirected my attention to trolling for cohos.

The one good thing about cleaning out the freezer is that it means it's time to go fishing and hunting in all seriousness. A few days later, with the season opening for Sitka blacktails, I was on Admiralty Island with my good pal, mountain guru and mad harmonica player Mike Janes. For Mike, hiking during the day on a mountain of the island some say has the densest concentration of brown bears was just too boring. He talked me into hiking during the night instead.

"People today have gotten soft!" he exclaimed as we paddled along the beach in the late evening. A brown bear, black in coloration, trudged along the shore in the opposite direction. After a month of feasting on salmon, its belly hung low, and it looked a bit like a big-bottomed hip-hop dancer in slo-mo. We stored our inflatable, along with survival gear, above a well-used bear bed. The calling of seagulls and bald eagles quieted to silence as we followed bear trails up a ridge.

"Hey, bear!" we yelled frequently. With all the ruckus we were making, I was fairly confident any bruin would have long since cleared out. Soon twilight came, forcing us to feel our way through brush, over fallen trees, and up slippery slopes until we had to get out headlamps. An hour later, at the edge of the subalpine, we lay down to sleep for a couple of hours. I daydreamed about fresh venison for less than a minute before conking out into oblivion. At three in the morning, we broke camp and crept up the mountain by headlamp. A night bird hurled by, bringing the silent forest alive for a moment. Even in the darkness, we could see deer sign was abundant. So was fresh bear sign. Our goal was to shoot two bucks close together, butcher them as quickly as possible, and get back down to the ocean.

At tree line, we moved as quietly as we could through the morning gloom. I made out a deer feeding a hundred yards away, so we hid behind a bit of brush and studied it with our scopes. It was a buck—and a big one at that. A little farther up the hill, two fork-horns, freezer-trophy bucks, appeared for a few moments before stepping out of view.

"If you can get a rest, take him," I whispered to Mike. Very slowly, as the big buck began following the other deer, Mike took off his backpack and rested his rifle. Before he could get a shot, the buck stepped out of view. We crawled through thigh-high vegetation until we were near the crest of the knoll. Mike was in the lead, and he looked back to let me know the deer were visible and he was going to shoot. I crawled a bit closer and to the side. His gun echoed, the big buck tumbled out of sight, and I slowly rose to my knees. One buck ran, but the other was stiffly walking away. I worked my bolt, and though my rest wasn't great, took a shot when the deer was broadside. It didn't appear to flinch and leapt out of view.

I was becoming increasingly alarmed after searching for fifteen minutes and not finding a trace of blood. I hiked to the rim of a bowl and scanned the area. A couple of deer looked up, but both were does. Cursing myself under my breath, I returned to where the deer had been. That's when I noticed an irregularity in the ground. I pushed the vegetation aside and, much to my surprise, looked down into sinkhole. There was a fat buck lying dead six feet below.

Mike and I butchered the deer together before slowly trudging down to the ocean. At home I packaged and canned meat. When MC wasn't looking, I shoved all the nonedible parts into a garbage bag and quickly threw it into the freezer. I couldn't help myself. There were a million potential uses: Halloween, Christmas, Easter, bar mitzvah, Ramadan, Druid rituals, weddings, baptisms, dance parties, fancy dinners, the zombie apocalypse, and even an anniversary or birthday present for MC. After all, nothing says "I love you" like a ball of venison fat and sinew.

CARIBOU SPOONS

ONCE, IN THE BROOKS RANGE, I carved spoons from a caribou antler to give to my three nieces. Any spoon bought at a store would do a better job of getting food into their mouths, but I wanted them to have something of caribou and wilderness, and to remind them there were other worlds out there in case they ever felt trapped.

Ten days or so before, I followed the fresh tracks of a large grizzly up a gorge toward a mountain pass. The wind was hard on my face, and the roar of a cascading stream blotted out all but my loudest warning calls. Hours wore on, and my nerves became increasingly frayed—at any moment, I expected to run into the bear. The tracks of two wolves appeared and then, strewn across the ground, lay a caribou calf. Blood and offal blackened the sand and gravel. Between the wolves and the bear, little flesh remained. I knelt, cupped the calf's face with my hand, and studied the black scree mountain slopes rising into dark clouds. A short while later, the bear appeared above the gorge, lumbering through rain and mist.

The next day, herds of caribou swirled over mountains and moved across valleys, leaving behind networks of trails. In creek and river bottoms, where dense deciduous brush offered good vantages for grizzlies and wolves to ambush, lay caribou bones and mostly eaten carcasses. One distressed cow ran toward me and then ran circles, as if it was looking for its calf.

When I returned home, I forgot to give my nieces those spoons. They disappeared, until two of them seemingly miraculously appeared on my bookshelf six summers later. I had four nieces and a nephew now, so I hung onto the spoons. The three girls had gotten to the point where they were going on their own adventures and could carve their own funny-looking eating utensils.

Not long after I found those spoons, my older brother, Luke, and his twelve-year-old daughter, Kiah, were nice enough to invite me along on a caribou hunt. It was Kiah's first journey into caribou country. Acting as a meat packer, I followed the two along alpine ridges and across tussocks. At the end of each day, we made dinner, laughed, and then sat quietly watching the sun set on ancient mountains. We lucked out and ran into three young bulls.

I had forgotten to bring plastic bags, and my pack became saturated with blood from the meat from the two caribou Luke and Kiah shot. After helping get the meat close to the road, I said goodbye. I planned to try to walk to the headwaters of the Yukon-Charley Rivers and then pack-raft to Circle. Kiah guilt-tripped me.

"Just come home with us," she said and shook her head in disbelief over how foolish I was being. I trudged away, looking back as my brother and his daughter hiked the opposite direction.

Two days later, smelling like a movable bear feast, I hiked over a knoll and saw the backsides of a sow grizzly and her big cub. I sat, hoping the wind wouldn't swirl my scent their way, and waited impatiently for them to move on. They followed caribou trails along the same ridge I needed to travel. When they were about four hundred yards away, I began trailing until I lost sight of them. Near dark I jumped a cow caribou and her calf in a band of scrub willows near a creek. They ran anxiously in circles as the last of the sunset reddened the mountains.

A blizzard rolled in that night. I wasn't prepared for deep snow, so I hiked out to the Taylor Highway and walked on the dirt road towards Eagle. A few moose hunters drove by and gave me apprehensive glances as I stood there with my thumb up. I didn't

Luke and Kiah with a Fortymile caribou.

blame them for not stopping. I looked and smelled pretty terrifying. Near dusk, while I was eyeing the woods for a decent camping spot, a truck pulled over and a man offered a ride. He was a carpenter from Fairbanks who'd wanted to show his family Dawson City and Eagle during a three-day weekend.

"I should ride in the back," I said. "I smell like a rotten caribou."

"Nonsense, hop in the cab," he said after introducing me to his wife and his three young daughters. In about five minutes, the girls went from being silent to excitedly telling me of the two lynxes they'd seen that day. The man and wife looked back, told stories about their adventure, and gently teased each other.

The next morning, I floated down the Yukon River towards Circle. There was no mail plane out of Eagle for a few days, and I had a bit of time before I needed to go back to work. Snow covered the mountains, and the yellow leaves fluttered in the wind as I drifted with the current. I thought of those caribou spoons, the struggles every animal shares, and how there could be no gift more wonderful or terrifying than trying to raise a young one.

THE CARIBOU OF
THE BROOKS RANGE

ONCE, WITH A FRIEND, I lay in the snow watching a herd of caribou mill in a valley in the Brooks Range. A dark wolf appeared and trotted the circumference of the herd.

"Maybe it'll push some our way," I said. Sure enough, a few caribou came plodding over a knoll as we readied our rifles. Late in the day, after we made it back to camp, we buried the skinned and gutted animals in the snow. My friend stared around at the icy mountains and the white expanse of the tundra. It was his first trip into the Arctic.

"Everything and their grandmas want to kill them," he said, referring to caribou.

I first ventured into the Brooks Range, the northernmost mountain range in Alaska, on a whim. I had ten days before classes began at the University of Fairbanks, so I borrowed an old truck from my friend Forest and drove north through the rolling hills and tundra. Near the continental divide, I forded the Dietrich River and followed a valley that led into the mountains. Three wolves woke me the first night. Two black and brown ones walked within yards as a big and nervous gray called them away. I continued west, mesmerized by the landscape, and encountered Dall sheep, other wolves, and grizzly bears. Classes began. A porcupine walked by my tent one morning. I was nearly out of food. If I didn't kill it, I'd have to begin the three-day trek back to the Haul Road. I watched him waddle away as I broke camp.

The following morning, I woke to a blizzard. A herd of fifty or so Dall sheep, looking like frozen statues, were bedded down nearby in the lee of the wind. When the storm let up, I hiked through snow, down into a valley, and around a grizzly eating the last of the year's low-bush blueberries. An hour later, in a willow thicket, I nearly stepped on a bear. It bluff charged multiple times, coming within what felt like inches, before running away.

When I made it back to Fairbanks, I was so haunted by the Brooks Range I could barely concentrate on my studies. My older brother, Luke, sensed my unease and made sure to go hiking and hunting with me as much as possible. We wandered the ridges and hills hunting grouse and trying to get a handle on how to go about getting a moose or caribou. We grew up in Southeast Alaska and were both relatively new to the Interior. Luke suggested we take a few days off in mid-October and drive to up the Haul Road to hunt. We enlisted Forest to join us on the endeavor.

None of us had really hunted the Arctic, though Luke had taken a caribou in the southern foothills of the Brooks Range with a bow the spring before. We began the drive north well before dawn. Multitudes of spruce grouse lined the side of the road collecting grit as we sped through hilly taiga. A big marten leapt across the road as we descended to the bridge over the Yukon River. When we got out to stretch our legs, we realized the temperature was below zero. We gassed up at Coldfoot and then drove up to the Chandalar Shelf and stared in amazement as thousands of caribou swirled with the hormonal excitement of the rut. Truck hunters dressed in white camo stalked the edge of the road with bows and arrows, pushing the caribou in circles. Red foxes gobbled gut piles in ditches. We nervously drove over Atigun Pass, looking for an area with fewer hunters. Caribou milled in scattered pockets on the North Slope, some under the pipeline. It's legal to hunt with a bow from the road, but rifle hunters have to hike in five miles. Forest and I sat in the truck watching Luke make a couple stalks on two different small groups of bulls. One giant, with three-foot tall, exceptionally palmated antlers, appeared to run Luke over while he was crouched behind a knoll.

"Well, it's not every day you get trampled by a caribou," I said, a little relieved after my brother stood up in disbelief. He'd missed a forty-yard shot at a young bull. Neither Forest nor I had a bow. All three of us agreed it would be a good idea to stretch our legs and make the trudge past the five-mile mark where rifle hunting is legal. The following morning, we glassed a few bulls we thought were in the rifle area, strapped on our snowshoes, and hiked west until, according to Luke's GPS, we were five miles from the road. Luke cautioned us as we trudged along.

"The big boys won't taste good, since it's the rut," he said. The caribou had moved on, leaving only tracks in the lonely, white monotony of the tundra. We glassed the area and, seeing no animals, decided to head back to the truck and try another spot that looked more promising. After a quick drive, we began another trudge as the sun set behind the mountains. Soon the aurora streaked across the icy blackness. At the five-mile mark, we made camp, complete with snow walls for protection from the wind. In the middle of the night, I woke to a cacophony of grunts, exhalations, and tendons clicking. I put on my headlamp and peered out at shadows in the darkness, milling and digging through the snow to browse lichens and grass.

Before sunrise, Forest and I streaked out of camp. Luke took a more casual approach and walked less than a quarter mile before shooting a young bull. I snowshoed miles and miles, blowing a few stalks in the open country. The sun had begun to dip behind the rugged mountains when I spotted a herd of sixty caribou. We had to be back the following day, so this would be my last chance. The final bit of the stalk was up a steep hill. When I reached the crest and lay down with my rifle resting atop my pack, I was panting and my heart was thundering. The caribou knew something was up and were moving quickly along a ridge about three hundred yards away. Slowly I worked the bolt and chambered a round. One by one, I watched the herd pass through my rifle's scope. I counted breaths and tried to will my heart to slow. Near the end of the herd was a four-year-old bull—the sort of animal that would be perfect for eating. I lined up on him, exhaled, and gently pulled the trigger. The

A bull caribou in the Brooks Range.

caribou fell, lifted its head momentarily toward the sky, and then lay motionless. The rest of the herd slowly trudged on, not bothering to look back, leaving the two of us alone in the white expanse. Soon his blood and musky smell had frozen all over me. I propped him so blood would drain out of his cavity and watched a speck that was my brother approach across the whiteness. After a smile and a word or two, we skinned the caribou and loaded it onto a sled.

Forest showed up to camp in the dark, covered in frost and icicles, dragging an old bull on a sled. In the months to come, it would take a bit of fortitude on his part to eat the rutty monarch. Beneath the aurora and mountains, exhausted but happy, we hauled the caribou back to the truck.

The Brooks Range had gotten a hold of all three of us. Over the years, we returned numerous times to hunt caribou in March and April. Each trip left us longing for more. Luke named one of his daughters after one of his favorite places in the Arctic. On one hunt, the only caribou we saw was a cow a wolf nearly chased through our camp while we were making breakfast. Neither Luke nor I could bring ourselves to shoot it. On numerous occasions we watched wolves stalking caribou. Once, a wolverine ran past our tent so focused on hunting Arctic ground squirrels that had just woken from hibernation that it didn't notice us or the three caribou we had buried in the snow.

After my first trip into the Brooks Range, I dreamed of traversing its 1,100-mile length by foot. I hesitated for five years. Finally, in March of 2009, I set out with my friend Ben on a month-long ski through the eastern portion. Not surprisingly, the trip was cold and challenging. Ben, perhaps from an infection due to frostbite, had to ski the last hundred miles to Kaktovik with a gruesome hole in his foot. A year later, I set out alone to traverse the central and western portion of the range. Once I passed the Nunamiut village of Anaktuvuk Pass, I began encountering caribou.

There's one young, lone bull that stands out in my memory. He'd been following me for a while as the sun cut through rain clouds, making certain features of shale-covered mountains glow. Each day for a week, I'd seen hundreds, even thousands of caribou. Great bulls, cows, yearlings, and calves wended across mountainsides and flooded across valleys. Most were traveling in groups between thirty and several hundred. The little bull and I made our way through clumps of waist- to chest-high willows toward a pass. It was the sort of travel that inspired me to yell, "Coming through!" frequently to warn bears.

"You shouldn't be alone," I told the caribou. I was getting a little tired of feeling like prey.

Early on during that same trip, in a narrow mountain ravine, I'd almost stepped on an old sow with two cubs that were nearly her size. I snuck away, but when she got my wind, she was less than pleased to be sharing the mountain with me. Another bear ran over my tent as I yelled and leapt off the vestibule. A large boar bluff charged near Agiak Lake. The dense willows along creeks and rivers offered perfect ambushes for bears and wolves. Studying all the caribou bones and carcasses that lay scattered, the phrase "corridors of death" kept popping up in my mind.

"Look, there's other caribou," I said, pointing to a scattered bunch. The young bull wandered out of sight but came back a few minutes later. In the evening, more scattered groups of caribou appeared. The little bull wandered farther away, until I lost sight of him.

At dusk, I finally made it out of the brush and found a good-looking spot to camp. I dropped my pack, stretched my back, and almost stepped on a bloody hindquarter of a caribou a grizzly had very recently torn off. Part of me wanted to eat it, but the bear was likely snoozing nearby on the rest of the carcass. I pulled out my pistol, slipped the straps of my backpack on, and hiked away into darkness. An hour later, the sound of tendons clicking and grunting made me pause. The shadows of caribou swirled away into the night.

Dear National Geographic,

Please Produce My Reality Show Idea

Today I offer a proposal more inspiring than your feature on the first ascent of Mount Everest, more dramatic than your television show *Wicked Tuna*, and even sexier than the December 1995 *National Geographic* cover shot of a chimpanzee looking for lice in Jane Goodall's hair. Before I delve too deeply into *our* future award-winning show, let me give a brief history of how my idea for the show *Toughest Alaskan* came to be.

A number of years ago, while attending the University of Fairbanks, I realized the rest of the state didn't think much of Southeast Alaska. When someone asked where I was from, they would often repeat "Ju-nooo!" like it was the cross between a satanic invocation and a swear word so terrible that if you muttered it too loud, a bar of soap would just miraculously appear in your mouth. My greatest point of contention wasn't the constant snickering or being refused every time I asked a girl out; no, it was the realization that people in the rest of Alaska believe that I, Juneauites, and other Southeast Alaskans weren't as tough as them. Which, if I'm honest, kind of hurt my feelings. After several weeks mostly spent writing poetry and sobbing on the phone to anyone who would listen, I set out to prove that we Southeasters are just as rugged and hard as any mad trapper living alone in the farthest reaches of the Arctic where the sun doesn't rise for 364 days each year.

This led to many interesting and fruitful conversations, such as the

My friend Geoff Cathy trying out for a spot on the *Toughest Alaskan* reality show.

old placer miner sucking back rot gut whom I met at the Howling Dog Bar in Fox.

"Give me a Mike's Hard Lemonade! No, I changed my mind. Make it a cosmopolitan!" I growled to the barkeep.

"You're from Southeast, aren't you?" the old miner asked and laughed.

I slammed my drink down, cursed when it spilled on my Patagonia jacket, and pointed to a scar on my face.

"You see this scar! No? Come closer then," I said until his tobacco-stained whiskers were just inches from my face.

"You mean that pimple?" he asked, confused.

"That's from the seventh time I was attacked by a bear in Southeast Alaska! How many times have you been attacked by a bear?"

"Once, and I've never been able to walk right since."

"That's nothing!" I said. "The fifth time I was attacked, after I headbutted the bear to death, a giant boulder fell on my arm. After several days of being trapped, I had to saw off my right hand with my right hand."

"Why didn't you just use your left hand?"

"Because I'm from Southeast Alaska!" I laughed. "And besides, I'd injured it doing yoga. You ever shoot a wolf while pissing in the Yukon River? I have. How about save a seal pup from a burning igloo, or sleep with a wolverine, or crash a small plane into an alien spacecraft bent on destroying Earth? I don't like to talk about it, but I've done all those things, and let me tell you another thing about Southeast Alaska—with all the rain, my thighs frequently chafe and my hair is always oily! I just can't seem to find the right pomade...what sort of products do you use?"

You probably get the gist of the dialogue. I had countless conversations like this during my time in the Interior and the North. After a while, I got so tired of all the hot air folks from up north were spouting that I decided to do something about it.

That's where *Toughest Alaskan* comes in.

The basic premise is that the toughest people from each region of Alaska are sent to compete against each other. I'm thinking seven episodes each season. The first episode will be a simple meet-and-greet potlatch in which each contestant brings their favorite dish. On the second episode, contestants will be subjected to a spaghetti-eating contest and voluntary wrestling matches involving giant foam fingers. For the third episode, I'm thinking K-Y Jelly wrestling with endangered marine mammals. This is a perfect way to make educating the public on climate change fun. The fourth episode will definitely involve roping musk ox and "slapping the bear." If you fail to agree to this, I'm dissolving our contract.

I'm thinking a combined hunt for Sasquatch and a sixty-degree-below-zero dance-off for the fifth episode. The sixth episode will be a watercolor painting contest.

The grand finale will be a mixture of the movie *Hunger Games* and

David Attenborough's *Planet Earth*. Contestants will be forced into a wilderness coliseum where the audience can enjoy the spectacular Alaskan scenery while people are forced to fight to the death. The last person alive will be the *Toughest Alaskan*—which I'm sure will be team Southeast—and will win something like a new iPhone with a free birdwatching app.

Please respond soon. If I don't hear from you, I will be forced to ask TLC or the Discovery Channel, and we both know they'll accept any idea as long as it has the word *Alaska* in it.

In fact, TLC and my lawyers are currently going over a contract for a reality show about a secret society that gets together once a month and juggles a variety of types of wild Alaskan animal droppings.

Sincerely,
Bjorn Dihle

YAKOBI ISLAND AND CROSS SOUND

SOMETIMES I DREAM of Yakobi Island and Cross Sound. The ocean undulates out of a gray horizon and crashes against black cliffs. A cannibalistic forest drips and moans in the grip of a storm. Halibut slime and salmon blood cover my rubber rain gear. King salmon streak through the water like rainbow-colored torpedoes. The sound of a friend's laughter rises above the wind and the chugging of a fishing boat's diesel engine, and I wake to my semi-suburban life feeling a mixture of dread and nostalgia.

Originally named Takhanes by the Tlingit, Yakobi Island is near the small fishing communities of Elfin Cove and Pelican. Its eighty-some square miles are uninhabited, except for brown bears, blacktail deer, and a handful of other species. To the north, Cross Sound and the Fairweather Range loom. The name of the range is a misnomer—Captain Cook, in 1778, had unusually good weather when he passed beneath and named the 15,300-foot crowning peak. Generally the region's weather is anything but fair. To the west, the big ocean stretches uninterrupted, hundreds of miles, all the way to Kodiak Island. To the east Lisianski Strait cuts a deep and narrow trench separating the island from Chichagof Island.

A job longlining for halibut and trolling for salmon with Joe and Sandy Craig brought me into that country a decade ago. In May, during my first season with them, Sandy pointed at Yakobi Island while a pile of halibut twitched in blood and slime on the deck of the *Njord.* Joe sat at the helm steering toward Elfin Cove.

"There in Surge Bay is where many think Aleksei Chirikov lost fifteen men in 1741," she said, gesturing with a circle hook in her hand. She went on to tell the story of the first contact between Russians and Alaskan Natives. The fifteen Russians, on two small boats, went missing while trying to make landfall. Their fate—whether drowning or death or capture by the Takhanes Tlingits—is debated. Sandy continued. "There's the lost village of Apolosovo in Surge Bay—I've gone looking for it many times. There's said to be a petroglyph there of a double-masted sailing ship, much like the vessel captained by Chirikov."

Each season we discussed the Chirikov expedition, the lost village of Apolosovo, and going to search Surge Bay for the petroglyphs. Seven years passed. Something—usually work—always came up to prevent us from making the journey. Finally Sandy had enough.

"We're doing it. Don't even try arguing. You've never won an argument with me," she said one May while we were camped with MC, my girlfriend, and Cal, Sandy's son, in the Stikine River Delta. In late June, I met Sandy in Elfin Cove. We ran up to the store to say hi to our friend JoAnn and grab a few last-minute provisions—herring and beer—before heading out on the glassy waters of Cross Sound. The Fairweather mountains stood blurred and white in the seventy-degree heat wave.

Joe was traveling with us in spirit. A year and a half ago, we had spread his ashes on a mountain he loved. Memories flooded back as we passed Yakobi Rock and neared the rocky entrance of Surge Bay. How many of Joe's spreads did I lose overboard while trolling that first season and then blame on pesky sea lions? There was that giant king that flopped off my gaff at Surge Bay while he was watching. There was no way I could blame a sea lion for that one. "I'll never be able to forget that," he said sadly. He never did. There was that bear with two cubs of the year that almost charged during a walk after a slow day fishing for cohos. There was that bull killer whale that swam docilely with a pod of Dall porpoises. There was the humpback whale that spy-hopped a sea otter out of the ocean. There was the baby killer whale that almost touched the *Njord* one morning while we were pulling a halibut longline. There was the big male bear that suddenly stood up ten feet away while I was sooty grouse hunting.

Sea otters, murres, murrelets, and loons parted as Sandy slowly motored towards the rocky shore of Yakobi Island. Salmon milled and splashed, waiting for the right moment to move into fresh water and spawn. Bob-o Bell, a hardcore fisherman, banjo player, and explorer, paddled a kayak toward us after we threw anchor. Normally it would be a little surprising to encounter someone alone out here, but seeing Bob-o felt oddly natural. After catching up, he asked if we'd seen Debra, his wife. I'd fished a few king openers with her and, knowing her character, figured she was busy climbing Mount Fairweather or challenging a brown bear to a mixed martial arts match.

I tied a rapidly deflating raft to a cliff and began meticulously searching different coves for the petroglyphs. A half hour later, I scouted a beach that offered a good landing for canoes. Seeing nothing after a quick sweep, I was about to turn back when I noticed a carving on an intertidal boulder. This was the place. This was where many people believe the lost village of Apolosovo was. The petroglyph-covered boulder seemed like a religious icon combined with a bulletin board. One depiction of a halibut radiated most clearly. Others were of salmon, circles, swirls, and the head of an eagle or thunderbird.

"Five times I've tried to find these petroglyphs," Sandy said quietly as she sat on a rock and studied the marks. At the northern edge of the cove, I happened upon the petroglyph of the supposed two-masted ship on a gray rock. We studied it carefully—its hull was much deeper than a Tlingit canoe's. It had four oars, a bow sprint, two ovals midship that could be interpreted as sails, an oval atop the stern, and what appeared to be an anchor line. Sandy came to a conclusion faster than I did.

"I think this has to be the second, smaller boat Chirikov lost. The four oars must mean four men, and it kind of looks like what others have called sails could actually be men," Sandy said. I agreed, but

Sandy Craig with a nice king salmon.

I also wondered if the carving was a depiction of a conglomeration of the *St. Paul* and the smaller boats. Whether the fifteen explorers drowned, were murdered, or were captured, I could only guess. What struck me most was how small, fragile, and barely visible these images were in relation to the rainforest and ocean. I wandered the woods looking for signs of a village. It had been more than two hundred years since the Takhanes people had disappeared from the island. With the severe weather and hungry rainforest, all signs of habitation had been absorbed back into the earth.

We hauled anchor, picking our way between rocks and out onto the big ocean to fish a few hours of the evening tide. The drag near Deer Harbor is notorious for brown bass. After releasing a couple, a rod bent deep. I eventually brought a lingcod, the hobgoblin of the fish world, to the surface. It spat out a bass it had been clinging to.

"That's dinner if we don't catch a king," Sandy said. The outer coast of Yakobi Island generally teems with fish in late June, so we were surprised after an hour of trolling without even a humpy to show for. At tide change, a rod began to hammer and line sang out. Sandy hooted and hollered as I played the king. Its dark back glittered as it sliced through the clear water. Shortly after we bled the fish and got our gear back down, a rod bent so deep that for a moment I wondered if we'd hung up on the bottom. The occasional tug told otherwise.

"This has got to be the granddad of lingcods!" I said, hanging on until the monster let go. I dropped another maimed brown bass in the bucket. We added a fat coho to the ice chest before heading into Surge Bay to anchor for the night.

Dawn came sunny and calm; a storm was supposed to roll in late in the day, so we hurried out to fish the morning. Sandy had recently bought her little boat in Juneau. Though it rode well and had character, it tended to break down. Sandy was adept at fixing it, but there were a thousand things we'd rather do than fight with a rebellious engine in stormy seas. A pole began hammering soon after we got our gear down. After landing the king, we added a handful of fat coho to the cooler. Sandy was planning on smoking the majority of them. Her smoked fish is some of the best in northern Southeast.

The last king of the morning was a hog. The rainforest mountains of Yakobi Island glowed in the dawn on one side and a wilderness of glaciers and mountain shone on the other.

In the early afternoon, we motored away from Yakobi Island. The wind began to pick up as we passed through the gut and into Elfin Cove's inner harbor. We visited with a few friends and grabbed a couple of things from Joe and Sandy's old house. That night, at the Craig's cabin in Gull Cove, we opened a bottle of whiskey and toasted the ghosts of the Chirikov expedition, the lost village of Apolosovo, and the folks we loved. A humpback whale lunge-fed in the still waters nearby.

We spent the morning halibut fishing and pulling shrimp pots in Icy Strait. After a couple hours, we had three twenty-five-pounders, my favorite size for eating, and a few dinners' worth of prawns. We processed the fish, vacuum packing some, and got a load in a brine to be smoked. At Elfin Cove, I said goodbye to Sandy and then begged a ride on a Beaver floatplane full of fishermen returning to their lives in big cities down south. I glanced back at Cross Sound—it was covered in rain clouds, and the ocean was full of whitecaps. Clouds swirled and parted to reveal green mountains during the eighty-mile

A view of Cross Sound and the Fairweather mountains as seen from the mountains above Elfin Cove.

flight to Juneau. We crossed northern Chatham Strait, and the jagged mountains guarding the Juneau Icefield appeared through the dark clouds. We touched down at the float pond in Juneau. The other passengers compared their number of missed texts, calls, and emails.

"I have 187 emails," one guy said and then stared sadly off into the distance. I paid my fare and drove to my little brother Reid's house for dinner. He'd caught a few nice halibut with our older brother, Luke, that morning. We settled down to eat fish, drink beer, and enjoy each other's company.

SHEEP COUNTRY

ONE YEAR IN EARLY SEPTEMBER, when birch forests glowed yellow and night temperatures dropped well below freezing, my two brothers and I began walking toward a seldom-visited mountain range in the interior of Alaska to look for Dall sheep. An eerie expanse of taiga, stunted and charcoaled from recent forest fires, filled valleys and lowlands below the ridge we followed. Wind-bleached moose and caribou antler sheds lay amidst rocks and lichens. The occasional willow ptarmigan croaked from patches of reddened willows. A network of caribou paths, some nearly as big as four-wheeler trails, fanned out through stunted willows and naked tundra. Reid pointed out a massive bull caribou. It shook its head, trying to rid its giant antlers of bloody strips of velvet. My brothers had done this exact same hunt eight years ago.

Eight hours after leaving the truck, we neared the summit of a six-thousand-foot mountain. A small herd of bull caribou swirled around us before disappearing over the top. For a country usually buffeted by winds, it was remarkably still. Snow clung to many of the surrounding mountains; it was late to be going into sheep country. We descended through a thick bank of fog, traveling by compass until the clouds cleared an hour later. Scattered groups of caribou grazing on willows, grasses, and lichens wandered valley and ridges. The sky gradually darkened; rain splattered the tundra. In twilight, we made camp above a field of tussocks.

I woke to heavy silence. Wet snow blanketed the tent. Reid and I slapped the nylon walls free, and the tent began to shake in the wind and hiss with falling snow. I lay in my sleeping bag listening to the weather until my craving for coffee was enough inspiration to venture out into the white world.

"It's getting nicer," I hollered as I filled the cook pot with snow and set it on my stove to boil. My brothers slowly emerged, grunting and grumbling like two bears that had just woken from hibernation. The snow gradually melted from the tundra, but the mountains remained white. Groups of caribou kept us company as we trudged through willows and tussocks. Often they'd come gallantly trotting, tendons clacking, and run circles around us. When they got our scent, they'd leap into the air, tilt back their heads—sometimes their antlers touched their backs—and nobly trot away. Rugged mountains grew closer, and all three of us felt the excitement of entering the desolate and beautiful world of sheep. We edged along a drainage, keeping to the willows for cover. Sheep have incredible eyesight and will spook from miles away.

"Sheep," Reid said, and he gestured at a snowy mountain five miles away. Luke got out his spotting scope and verified that the tiny off-white specks were indeed sheep. We snuck across to the other side of the drainage and crept along just inside the edge of willows.

"There are six, but I'm not seeing any adult rams," Luke said when we were a few miles closer.

We glassed every bowl, ravine, and slope and slowly hiked deeper into the mountains. Though we saw no more sheep, we were far from being alone. Caribou filled the valley and surrounding drainages. Once, we sat down and watched seven giant bulls approaching. They were so busy feeding that, seemingly oblivious, they walked within yards. A golden eagle flapped its wings from its perch at the base of a mountain. One of the more impressive raptors, it's a formidable predator of young sheep, mountain goats, and caribou calves. On a mountain goat hunt years ago, a golden eagle had buzzed me and

Reid while we were traversing a knife-edge ridge with a multi-thousand-foot fall on either side. I couldn't help but wonder if the bird was thinking about trying to knock us off into the abyss, the same way it would hunt a sheep or goat.

"Looking pretty skinny in the sheep department, but that's what we expected," Luke said in the late evening when we'd reached the head end of the valley and were setting up camp.

This trip was a last-minute decision. Two days previously, we had returned from a sheep hunt in the eastern Alaskan Range. We'd budgeted nine days for that hunt, but I'd lucked out and taken a beautiful ram on opening day. Our original plan was to try for caribou after the Alaskan Range sheep hunt before returning home, but caribou season was still days away from opening. In the time we had to spare, we decided to trek to Luke and Reid's old sheep grounds, even though the biologist who sealed my horns had cautioned us.

"There're very few sheep there. I recently flew a survey of the entire range and only saw two full-curl rams," he'd told us. Despite the low probability of getting a ram, we agreed it would be an adventure and a fun way to whittle away the days until caribou season.

"Well," I said, boiling a cup of tea and staring up at the darkening mountains, "even if we don't get a sheep, I'm happy to be in such beautiful country."

It was well before dawn when we shouldered our packs and began climbing an icy scree slope up into the mountains. Snow plastered the top of the ridge. Barren valleys and lonesome taiga stretched in every direction below.

"Sheep," Reid said, gesturing towards a small herd of ewes and lambs grazing in a valley floor. We worked our way north along the snowy ridge, glassing as we went. The sun crept above the horizon, and a breeze whispered against our wind-chapped faces.

"Sheep," Reid said an hour later, pointing at a distant ridge.

"They're rams!" Luke whispered, staring through his spotting scope. We debated how, and if it was possible, to get to the herd. Even if we could reach them, there was a high probability that none would be full curl. One option was to follow a long series of jagged ridges and come down on them—it's always best to come from above on sheep—but the terrain looked impossibly steep and exposed. The other option was to descend a mountain, use a drainage for cover, and get below the herd. There was too good of a chance of getting in trouble if we tried traversing the ridge, so we decided on the second plan, even though we agreed our chances of success were poor. After picking our way carefully through steep scree, we ran down a snowy slope, upsetting a flock of rock ptarmigan as we went. Luke crawled to a knoll and used his spotting scope to look the sheep over. Pikas, little mountain rodents, chirped from their homes in piles of rocks.

"The ram that's highest looks like it might be full curl! The other ram with him might be too!" he whispered. We continued down the drainage and stopped when we noticed a subadult ram staring at us from a nearby slope. After ten minutes, he made his way in a slow and dignified manner over a ridge toward the rest of the rams. A forest of stunted black spruce and willows grew up out of the bottom of the drainage. It was getting late, and the thought of spending the night out in the snow and potentially stormy weather was far from appealing.

"I don't think we really have a chance either way," Reid said. The two biggest rams were a few miles away. Between them and us were six smaller rams. "If we go up at them, we'll be totally exposed, but there's always that tiny percentage of a chance the boss ram will let us walk within range."

"We could try climbing another mountain and seeing if we can loop around on them. I don't know if we have enough daylight though," I said trying to sound cavalier but hoping my brothers would consider it a ridiculous plan. They muttered something about being in it for the fitness, and the next thing I knew, we were climbing up thousands of feet of loose boulders. At the top, we belly crawled through snow and peered over the edge. Five hundred yards away lay two rams chewing their cuds. After a quick look through the scope, it was obvious neither was legal. The boss ram and another big ram were still a few miles away. Picking our way through shifting rocks, snow, and ice, we continued. An American kestrel—a small falcon—swooped along the ridge and hovered above. An hour later, when we were out of view of the two big rams, we began descending a series of sheep trails into a valley.

"They're just over this next mountain," Luke said. It suddenly dawned on me that we had a high probability of pulling the stalk off, a thought that seemed so crazy I pushed it aside. Instead, with my heart pounding and lungs straining, I focused on trying to keep up with my brothers as they rapidly ascended a slope covered in scree and snow. We paused at the top of the ridge, not far from where we'd last seen the two rams. An electric pulse throbbed in the crisp air. Fresh sheep tracks wended along the snowy ridge. Reid belly crawled through snow and peered over the edge.

"They must be over the next bump. They're going to be close," he whispered. Luke sat down and refused to go on.

"Just go with Bjorn," he said. "I'm so jacked up right now, I'd likely tell you to shoot even if it isn't quite full curl."

Reid and I slowly and somewhat painfully crawled over scree and boulders. The first ram came into view, and my heart did a few somersaults before thudding out of control. He was grazing sparse patches of grass, with his head facing away from us. I checked the distance with Luke's range finder. "Two hundred yards," I mouthed to Reid. Slowly, I set up the spotting scope. His horns were close, but I was pretty sure he wasn't legal. I shook my head and mouthed, "Seven-eighths." We slunk forward a few yards and, by barely peeking above a small boulder, spotted the other ram. His horns were much bigger; it was obvious he was the boss.

"Is he full?" Reid hissed after I squinted through the spotting scope for a few minutes.

"Probably, but I wouldn't swear to it," I whispered, then I passed him the scope.

"I think he's full, but I'm not entirely sure. What do you think?" he asked. We'd had this exact same conversation five days ago when I was lined up on a ram. Mine had turned out to exceed a full curl by quite a bit. Punishment for shooting a ram that's not full can be severe; just the tragedy and embarrassment of having your meat and horns taken away was enough to make me hesitant to pull the trigger. Now, minutes passed while Reid and I whispered back and forth. The boss ram's horns certainly looked legal, but what if our eyes were playing tricks on us? The two sheep began walking away, grazing as they went. Luke couldn't take it anymore and crawled over.

"He's full curl," he said after a quick glance through the scope.

My brothers and me with a nice ram taken deep in the Interior of Alaska.

"Bjorn, would you shoot him?" Reid asked.

"I don't know," I said, not wanting to send my little brother to jail. He's too pretty for prison.

"He's full," Reid whispered and rested his rifle on a boulder and chambered a round. At the crack of the shot, the sheep stumbled, ran a few yards, and fell dead atop a patch of snow. The other ram turned and sprinted toward his fallen companion, paused, and then touched his nose against him. A moment later, he fled into the mountains. Without a word, Reid ran down the slope and knelt next to the ram. He smiled up at us after examining its horns. They were big, wide, and well beyond legal. Luke sat down in a daze and studied the sheep. Later, he'd tell me that this was the exact same ridge, within a few hundred yards, where he'd shot his sheep eight years previously. The power and intimacy of the ram and mountains were palpable as we knelt. With reverence and a touch of sadness, we prepared to butcher.

"He's such an amazing animal. I'm not sure I ever want shoot another," Reid said. Luke and I felt similarly; there's something so special about taking a sheep that it would be just fine if it was only a once-in-a-lifetime experience.

It was late in the day; eight hours had passed since we'd begun the stalk. Getting back to camp could be problematic if a storm materialized—a frequent occurrence in this country. Quickly, we divided the meat and horns and began the long trek back. It was nearly dark when we crested the mountain rising above the valley where camp was. Exhausted but happy, we descended by the light of our headlamps.

Caribou and an icy wind kept us company as we trudged back toward the road. The first night, we camped in the lee on a mountain ledge. In the early morning, while it was still dark, I woke to the howling of a wolf. Caribou milled nervously, and a golden eagle flew over close enough to make out individual feathers. Toward dusk, we neared the dirt road where we had left our truck. I paused and looked back at a wild, open expanse leading to the white mountains of sheep country. The peaks grew dimmer until only their silhouettes remained. Tingling, I caught up with my brothers, and together we walked the last miles to the truck.

GRIZZLY COUNTRY

MY DAD FIRST TOOK ME and my two brothers to Admiralty Island when we weren't much bigger than tadpoles. There are a lot memories from that trip: giant spruce and hemlock trees, ravens speaking their ancient language, eagles gliding above a stream teeming with pink salmon, the seemingly impenetrable jungle surrounding the creek, a brown bear—which, at the time, I thought was a big, weird-looking dog—ghosting into the salmonberry bushes, the tracks of deer, and my yearning to become a hunter, to name a few. But the memory that stands out most was of a mostly eaten carcass in a stream. My dad looked at it as salmon struggled to spawn around its decomposing flesh.

"It's a brown bear," he said.

Almost thirty years later, I hurriedly gutted a Sitka blacktail buck as the setting sun bathed the green mountains of Admiralty in soft light. A few hundred yards away, my older brother, Luke, was working on another deer. Reid, the youngest, had taken a big three-by-three and was out of sight near the top of the mountain. I skinned the hindquarters, broke the brisket, propped the ribs open to cool, and hiked over to Luke. A faint but terrible bellowing cut through the still evening.

"Do you hear that?" I whispered as Luke and I climbed a steep slope.

"It sounds like an old woman screaming," Luke said.

"She's screaming close to where Reid ought to be," I said.

"Wait," Luke said, cocking his head towards the sound. "I think that's Reid."

"There's a bear to your right!" Reid yelled down. Our little brother is a cool customer. He's only yelled one other time in his life, shortly after he lost a big halibut. We were a little surprised to see him so worked up. After gutting the deer he shot, he'd walked a short way to see if he could see us.

"Luckily I grabbed my pack at the last moment. When I looked back, there was a bear on the deer," he said.

"Well, let's go teach it a lesson," I said, thumping my chest. We could just make out the bear seventy yards away in the dusky light. "I got this," I told my brothers. I yelled and stepped forward, screaming and jumping up and down like a two-year-old having a tantrum. The bear took two steps toward us and flexed its forearms.

"I'm not sure he's getting your lesson," Reid said.

"Give me another chance," I said, out of breath and sweaty. I began howling and thrashing.

"He's not looking that impressed," Luke said as I panted in exhaustion. We decided not to fire a warning shot as the bear was acting tense enough to charge. None of us wanted to kill a brown bear or haul the hide and skull down for Fish and Game and go through the paperwork. Soon all we could make out was a shadow in the darkness. We got out headlamps and hiked for a bit before trying to get a few hours of sleep. At first light, we hauled the two remaining deer out of there.

I have no shortage of respect for brown bears. There's no other animal in the woods that inspires a similar sense of awe, fear, and fascination. I've spent a lot of time, often alone, in bear country. Most encounters end with a butt-end view of a bruin rapidly exiting the area. There have been some encounters that were less than pleasant, but I've only come close to shooting a bear a couple times. There was the grizzly that was on my tent—with me in it—in the Brooks

Range. I'd been asleep, and when I leapt out yelling with a cocked pistol, I wasn't even sure what was going on. Before I could even shoot, the bear exhaled and sprinted off, running over my tent in the process. I'm pretty sure a bear on Admiralty thought I was a deer or something else it wanted to kill. I didn't shoot, even though I probably should have. On another occasion—the first time a bear charged me—I only had pepper spray. I was walking into a stiff wind, so the spray was worthless. The grizzly came close to knocking me down, then bounced away, and then bluff charged again. The bear could have made contact twice by the time I got my spray unclipped. If I'd had a pistol, I would haven't hesitated shooting. I got lucky, and the bear ran away after a series of bluff charges.

Often, especially when I'm traveling alone in grizzly country, I'll ask if it's okay to camp in a certain place. In the morning, I'll offer thanks for not being killed during the night. Another quirk I've developed from bear encounters is that sometimes when I'm at home, I'll hear a noise, do a somersault, arm myself with whatever is handy—usually a book or spatula—and attack the closest thing at hand, which is most often my tiny golden retriever, Fen. Inevitably, this ends with me throwing my back out, Fen wrestling me, and my gal, MC, muttering something about someone needing a psychiatric evaluation.

Brown bears bring out no shortage of strangeness in people. For the last six years, I've guided folks and a few film crews who wanted to look at or film brown bears. It's been pretty cool to get a feel for the personalities of individual bears. One bear who was a cub when I first met her had her first litter of cubs the winter of 2016. Equally as exciting, that summer I was offered the chance to become a Hollywood star.

"Hi, sport," a reality television producer said over the phone. "Are you interested in being part of a team that tries to track down the biggest brown bear in the world? Some say it's not even a bear! They say it's, like, fourteen feet tall!"

"Where's this 'bear' supposed to live?" I asked, beginning to shake with excitement. Maybe a brown bear had successfully mated with a tiger, creating a "tigear" or "beager," and I was about to be offered a ticket to the Kamchatka Peninsula.

"On the island of Angoon," the producer said.

"You mean the village of Angoon on Admiralty Island?" I said.

"What? Yeah. The village of Angoon," he said.

"Who gave you this exciting information?" I asked.

"The Langat people."

"I never heard of the Langat people. Do you mean Tlingit?" I asked. The conversation grew increasingly strained. The producer said something about isolated DNA and there being some sort of super bear near Angoon. Like all critters, except maybe porcupines, bears thoroughly enjoy humping, and they don't discriminate much when they're horny. A few times during the spring, I'm pretty sure a couple bears tried to make the moves on me. When they groaned, it sounded remarkably like, "Why can't I quit you?" With how free-spirited bears are, I highly doubt there's any genetically isolated individuals on Admiralty.

"Whoever told you this is pulling your leg," I told the producer. "The biggest bears are out on Kodiak and the Alaska Peninsula."

My life dream is to be cast as the villain in a James Bond movie, but I was tired of all the nonsense being perpetuated about bears. It's like what Allen Hasselborg, the bear man of Admiralty Island, said about so many people's apparent need to dress up bear stories—the truth is plenty interesting already. Still, a small part of me died when I declined to be on the show. I so wanted to almost kill James Bond and come within a few millimeters of taking over the world.

It wasn't the first time a reality television producer had made a strange request to me concerning brown bears. Years before, while working as a guide and packer on a show, the producer got upset when I informed him there was about a zero percent chance we'd be able to get an aggressive bear encounter on film. What really seemed to tick him off the most was I wouldn't even try to make it happen.

"I really need that shot!" he said, pouting as we walked through an estuary on Chichagof Island. Ever resourceful, he made a few calls on the satellite phone and then ordered the "contestants" to act like they were being attacked. Those poor guys were attacked nearly a dozen times by imaginary bears in the four days of filming.

It's not just film crews. Plenty of individuals have strange bear fantasies or want bears to do strange things to them. For instance, once I guided a French couple who wanted to swim with sea lions and be charged by a brown bear.

"How about we just look at them," I suggested. The woman gave me a nasty look that, much like the idea of doing yoga in public, deeply threatened my masculinity. For a half second, I wondered if I was being a sissy for being afraid to swim with a half-ton sea lion in icy water. Being charged by a bear might sound cool, but honestly, it's not good for one's mental health. Out on Admiralty Island, after a few days in the rain and wind, a medium-sized bear stood up from the rye grass thirty yards away and huffed. I got ready in case it charged and then apologized for startling it. After a few tense moments, it dropped to all fours and charged off in the opposite direction. I looked over my shoulder to see the French couple standing in a fetal position and nearly pressed against me. They mentioned something about being ready to go back to town.

Perhaps the strangest character I've encountered was a woman camped alone on a salmon stream on Admiralty Island. She was a professor from back east who was planning to spend the summer trying to answer philosophical question like whether or not humans belong in the bear's world, writing poetry, and doing other stuff that kind of went over my head. She lectured me and my clients about bears and told us we would see none before she climbed over her electric fence and back in her tent. We moved to an estuary a few miles away, sat still for an hour, and were soon watching a number of bears fish, walk the shore, and nap. Surprisingly, there's only been one definitive bear fatality on Admiralty in the last hundred years. I wondered if the professor would become the second. Camping on a salmon stream during spawning season is akin to sleeping on the bears' dinner table. Thankfully, she tired of the rain and bears not acting the way she wanted them to. She abandoned her project, attempted to travel the well-used Cross Admiralty Canoe Route, and ended up having to be rescued.

I find some people's lack of interest in bears equally baffling. One example was a family with two boys who were around the ages of seven and nine. We were waiting for a couple of hours in an estuary that received few human visitors and had yet to see a bear. The boys passed the time looking dejected and throwing pebbles at their boots.

A brown bear photographed at the Pack Creek Observatory on Admiralty Island.

I noticed a flash of brown in the beach grass forty yards away. Soon a large blocky head rose above, and a groggy bear who'd been napping clambered to all fours. The parents hissed with excitement. The kids sighed and continued tossing pebbles. The bear, a large male, turned and began ambling towards us. The boys whined about being bored and continued throwing pebbles as the bear, oblivious of us, came within thirty yards. I said hello and the bear paused and then, in very dignified manner, slowly turned and walked away. Once it was hidden by the brush, it charged away. I was excited, and I know the other two adults were too. I'm not sure the boys ever looked up. The father apologized.

"They don't know what to do without their electronics," he whispered, sadly shaking his head.

For the last deer hunt of 2016, my dad and I went to Admiralty Island. Even though it was mid-November, bear sign was still plentiful, so we stuck together. Other hunters had already hit the area. We saw few deer, but during a stormy evening, two bucks appeared in the misty woods. After a few moments of violence and excitement, we knelt over their bodies and thanked them. We worked quickly, glancing over our shoulders as we skinned and sliced to make sure a bear hadn't snuck up on us. Our packs bit into our shoulders as we hauled the meat down the mountain. I thought of how my dad had hunted this island for forty years and how when I was a tyke on my first trip here the woods had felt impenetrable. The idea of encountering a bear and hunting deer seemed magical. In the thirty years since, I'd explored the island from its northern tip to its southern limit. I'd made journeys into its interior and kayaked its circumference. Even after losing track of the number of deer I'd shot and bears I encountered, I still felt a similar sense of wonder and awe as I had when I was four years old. A branch snapped, the wind made the forest creak and moan, and I focused as one should always do while on Admiralty. Straining our eyes and ears, my dad and I slowly worked our way down through the dark woods.

FISHLOVE

I REMEMBER MY FIRST DATE. I was walking down the boardwalk of Elfin Cove—a quaint fishing community in northern Southeast Alaska—in my rubber rain gear, about to go out to the outer coast for the big king salmon opener, when it happened quite unexpectedly. A woman who bore an uncanny resemblance to Long John Silver whistled.

"Hey, sugar stack! I'm going to throw you over my shoulder and take you down to my fish hold!"

"Gee, thanks! But shouldn't I talk with your father first?" I asked. Naturally I was flattered, but things got a little weird when she pulled out a gaff and started chasing me. She yelled something about how good my bibs looked and how the smell of my unwashed sweatshirt, coated in weeks' worth of halibut slime, was driving her as mad as a rutting bighorn in a barnyard. Then her peg leg caught in a crack, and she sprawled out on the dock. She coughed out a softball-sized wad of chewing tobacco and a lingcod then looked up with a passion and tenderness I'll never forget. She whispered something that sounded like a sea lion belching, and for a second, I thought that I could spend the rest of my life with this woman. I'd heard a lot of horror stories about dating, but so far things seemed be going all right. When she pulled out a lead pipe—recently used to dispatch a few thousand halibut—I knew that old saying "love can be dangerous" was true. I suddenly realized I'd become a victim of "fishlove."

A recent issue of *Today's Journal of Fisherman's Psychology and Relationship Advice* says that fishlove is becoming so prevalent that many men are afraid to go to their favorite fishing holes. The article states that women can't resist men who fish, especially when they're wearing chest waders. Add a creel and a hat rimmed with an assortment of flies that look like waterfowl sluiced at close range with an 8 gauge shotgun, and a fellow will get fishcalled endlessly.

Not all victims of fishlove have had their teeth knocked out, their hands broken, and been given an incurable rash resembling elephant barnacles and a sculpin. More traumatizing are the psychological effects. Even though I eventually had to shove her into the water because of how complicated our relationship became, it took me a long time to get over Long John Silver. Many fishermen are so tired of being objectified, they've created support groups where they can express their feelings about being treated like trophy fish. Others have what *Fisherman's Psychology* calls Post Traumatic Fishlove Disorder. Many have experienced "fish it on the run" and spend their lives being bitter after being left for younger and better-looking fishermen. The heart is a watery abyss.

I attended one such meeting at my friend Jesse "The Fish Doctor" Walker's garage. We dressed in bear skins and sang our secret chant, which sounds oddly like a Tina Turner song. Matt "The King Salmon Slayer" Thrasher was brought up. Thrasher fishes and hunts harder than just about anyone I know. He moved to Alaska a while ago. Eventually he tired of suffering fish harassment and returned to his native state of Maryland a few years back. Only wanting to hunt and fish or talk about hunting and fishing, he inevitably became good friends with the likes of Jesse and me. Naturally we were worried when he left Alaska. Not long after, a girl saw him emerge from the woods with a deer over one shoulder, a fishing pole in one hand, and a string of trout in the other. In a heartbeat, she was in fishlove. She hit him with her truck, threw him in the bed, and the next thing

Matt Thrasher popping the big question to Kelsey, his bride-to-be, with the Chilkat Mountains in the background. (Photo courtesy of Jesse Walker)

Thrasher knew, he was standing at a barbecue, wearing an apron that said "Property of Kelsey," and cooking surf and turf for her family.

Soon after attending the support group, I was flying across the continent with my girlfriend, MC, for Matt and Kelsey's wedding. Thankfully MC got over her fishlove for me years ago. She occasionally gaffs or whips me with a fly rod in a nostalgic attempt to relive the good times we shared when we first met. These days we have a healthy relationship that involves a strained silence, the occasional sigh, and the mandatory once-a-year date night that inevitably results in staying home and watching a B movie on Netflix. Sometimes I worry she's discontent, especially when she studies fishermen motoring by with binoculars and mutters about how few fish I've recently caught.

In Maryland, as we watched Matt and Kelsey get married, I couldn't be happier for the two of them. Kelsey still has not gotten over her fishlove for Thrasher. Whenever MC and I hang out with the two, Kelsey whispers things like, "I just love how Matt smells like bait. It makes me wild!" The ceremony's crowning touch was after their vows, when the Fish Doctor released a flight of doves. The newlyweds took a break from smooching to pull out shotguns and ensure that dove potpie would be served at the reception.

MC and Fenrir with a grayling on the Yukon River.

SISU

LATE-SEASON BLACKTAIL hunting in Southeast Alaska can be a dark, tangled, and sometimes dangerous affair. On the northern islands—Admiralty, Baranof, and Chichagof—there's a decent chance of stumbling into a jungle wookie (cool slang for brown bear). These encounters offer a respite to the lonesome and tedious hours, days, and months many hunters spend each year studying botany while in pursuit of game. In early November of 2015, my two brothers, our dad, and I decided to fly into one of the many lakes on Admiralty Island, rent a Forest Service cabin, and celebrate Dad's sixty-fifth by wandering around the woods in hopes of bumping into a buck or two.

The morning of our departure was gray and drizzly but unseasonably warm, as it was in all of the state. A late-season fly-in hunt to a lake can be a gamble. A cold snap that freezes a lake means a hunter has to seek an alternative sort of extraction—generally, that means walk out to the ocean. Our forecast was calling for rain for a week, so we weren't too worried. The Beaver floatplane cut across Stephens Passage, up a dark valley of Admiralty Island, and over the black water of the lake. The pilot, after checking for submerged logs, landed into the wind. A few minutes later, we'd unloaded our kit and listened to the quiet come back to the land as the whine of the plane disappeared into the gray. Deer are the one species in Alaska you can hunt the same day you fly. Luke and Reid, my two brothers, were off into the woods like a couple of wolverine in heat as soon as we hauled the last load to the cabin.

"They're maniacs," Dad said. Clouds swirled to reveal a jagged mountain covered in fresh snow. Perhaps a bear or two, fat from gorging on salmon runs, were asleep in their dens on the slopes above.

"I'll give the base of that mountain a look," I said. "Unless you want to go there."

"I'll head up the hill behind the cabin," Dad said.

"Let's hope they're in the rut," I said. I shouldered my pack and climbed up a steep brushy hill. I prefer taking deer in the early season when they're fat, tasty, and high in the mountains. August had been kind. By the middle of the month, the mountains had yielded three bucks for my freezer. With only one tag left, I'd kept my rifle stored for the last few months. I passed through a series of big muskegs, taking note of fresh deer and bear sign. One set of tracks was from a medium bear that had passed through during the last day or two. In some areas, there was more bear than deer sign, although for the most part it was a few weeks old. Being quiet in bear country can be counterproductive. That's another reason why I prefer early season hunting—there's better visibility in the alpine. Even then, running into bears is common enough. I hiked through a stand of big spruce and hemlocks, found a good vantage point, and blew my deer call. None of my family has ever been that into calling. My two brothers are like restless wolves. Sitting still is not natural for them. They were born to stalk and chase. I'm similar, but I'd describe myself as more of a large, deranged, fidgety marmot who wants to be a wolf. We've all had success with the call, but on Admiralty you never know what you might call in.

After a half hour, the woods were getting darker. I wanted to get back before dusk—what's a hunting trip with a cabin if not an excuse to drink an extra cocktail or two? In the gloom, a large deer ghosted through the brush unaware of me. I quietly worked my bolt, brought my rifle to my shoulder, and squinted through my scope. It froze and cocked its head back to look at me. A doe. I lowered my rifle. I hoped that the next four days would offer something with antlers. I met Dad at the cabin at dark.

"Nothing," he said, shrugging. "There was some good sign about seven hundred feet up."

I lit the lantern and cursed Reid and Luke. They should get back so I could crack a beer. Shortly, they arrived empty-handed. I made dinner as they sat around talking about past hunts, big bucks taken, and big bucks that got away.

"We're going to have to work for our deer," Luke said.

The next morning, we went our separate ways. I climbed up into the fog to about seven hundred feet and began to see pockets of good sign. A deer popped out from behind the tree thirty yards away, froze, and looked up at me. I wiped my scope, studied its head, and saw acorn-like antlers—a button buck. I've always been a freezer-trophy hunter, and this little guy would be delicious, but I hesitated. We had three more days to hunt. The deer stared at me for a half minute before slowly walking away and disappearing in the brush. I hunted hard until dusk, passed on a doe, and then beelined toward the cabin. In thick brush, I jumped a large deer. By the time I had my rifle up, all I could see was the side of the belly and haunch as it thundered off into the woods.

Dad hadn't seen any deer, Reid had passed on three does, and Luke staggered in late by the light of his headlamp.

"Your pack looks heavy," Dad said. Luke smiled sheepishly before telling us about his day. After passing on a couple does, he'd been hiking along the side of a ridge when he came to the edge of an open area. He said what felt like a force field prevented him from taking another step, so he froze and waited. After a few minutes, a nice buck appeared on the other side of a ravine. Luke got in position for a shot, and the deer disappeared for a moment into the brush. A moment later, a large deer appeared, and Luke shot. While he was walking toward where he last saw the animal, a buck stepped out and eyed him for a second too long.

"You punk," Reid said. "You had to go and shoot two." In the dark, we rigged up a hang and hauled the meat from the two deer fourteen feet off the ground. We fried up the two hearts and some

Dad after a successful late-season hunt on Admiralty Island.

backstrap to go with pasta for dinner that night.

The next morning, Dad and I heard a shot five minutes after Reid left. I walked down the trail a few hundred yards and found Luke and Reid in a meadow admiring a nice buck. Its neck was swollen, and it had very little in its stomach, but it still had a good cushion of fat on its hindquarters and back. I quelled my jealousy, hiked to the top of a ridge, and explored all the way to tree line. A few deer ghosted out of the fog, but none were animals I wanted to shoot. Reid was sitting alone on the cabin steps when I walked in. There seemed to be an inordinate amount of game bags hanging in the tree.

"How'd it go?" he asked.

"No luck," I said. "How was the rest of your day?"

"Oh," he said humbly but with a small smile, "I shot another buck."

After hauling his deer back and hanging it, he decided to walk back down the trail toward the gut pile. Ten minutes later, he saw what he assumed was a stump, even though it sure looked like a deer on the hillside above. He lay down behind a rock, took a rest, and peered through the scope. It was another fat buck.

"Those'll probably be the two easiest bucks I'll ever get," he said.

Dad showed up well after dark. He still hadn't seen a deer and was feeling a little defeated.

"I think I might hang out at the cabin tomorrow," he said.

"Come on out with me, and we'll go get skunked together," I said.

"I don't want to ruin your chances," Dad said.

"I've been doing a pretty good job of doing that on my own," I said.

"I'll go with you," Reid said, and Dad reluctantly agreed.

I spent the following day wandering the woods and hoping a nice deer would present itself. I covered miles of open stands of woods without seeing anything besides a small doe. I was doing my best to be philosophical, but if I'm honest, I was a little bothered about the prospect of going home without a deer. This was my chance to add more venison to the freezer. Almost as bad, Luke and Reid would make me even more of the butt of their jokes for a long time to come. I hiked through the gloomy forest, looking and listening for bears, until I came upon the cabin illuminated by a lantern. A massive rack lay on the bench outside the door. I assumed Luke, with proxy tags, had taken the deer. It was, quite possibly, the biggest set of Sitka blacktail antlers I'd seen.

"Dad shot it," Reid said, coming outside with a huge smile. Dad shrugged. Reid and Dad had hiked to the far side of the lake and crept up into the hills. They attempted a stalk on a smaller deer, but it vanished before they were able to get a good look at it. A short while later, they came into country thick with sign. Peering around a hillock, Dad spied a big buck looking his direction fifty yards away. It knew something was up. Quietly he worked the bolt of the .338 he'd hunted Admiralty with for four decades, took a rest on the side of the mound, and shot. The buck crashed a few yards before lying still in a muskeg pool.

The next day, Reid and Luke flew home on a Cessna 180—Luke was adamant about not missing his daughter Adella's birthday. It was a few days away, but weather delays in late fall in Southeast Alaska are common. Dad and I were scheduled to get picked up the next morning. I hunted hard, and as the hours whittled away and I encountered no deer, I felt more and more defeated. At that point, I would have been happy to harvest a doe. The meat means everything to me, not the size of the antlers. I just rarely shoot anything female, mostly because it's better for populations. It was approaching dusk by the time I got cut off by a big avalanche chute and had to walk to the bottom of it. The cabin was a mile away, and it would be dark by the time I arrived. I looked up at the dark clouds moving over the black forest. The lightness of my pack felt heavy. I thought about *sisu*, a Finnish concept our dad had taught me and my brothers. It basically means never giving up, no matter how hard and crappy things seem. To the last moment, even if you're getting beat and there's no hope, you keep on trying. A moment later, I was hiking back up into the woods. I saw what looked like a deer bedded down on the hillside. I made an impressive, elaborate stalk, but the deer turned out to be a rock. I chuckled and began walking back toward the lake in the deep gloom. At least my failure to get a deer ended with a bit of comedy. Suddenly, I made out the outline of a deer ghosting through the woods. In one motion, I quietly worked the bolt, brought the rifle to my shoulder, and fired. My initial excitement and sense of relief quickly faded to sadness as I sat next to the young buck as its life shivered away. By the light of my headlamp, I butchered the deer and then worked my way down through the woods.

CPSIA information can be obtained
at www.ICGtesting.com
Printed in the USA
BVHW01s1932280118
506269BV00004B/6/P